Some preliminary thoughts about this book

A few days after the crucifixion of Jesus Christ, two men were walking and talking on a road from Jerusalem to Emmaus. Luke records in the last chapter of his Gospel (Luke 24:13-32), that as they walked, the resurrected Jesus joined them, and in response to their comments, He said:

> **O foolish men and slow of heart to believe all that the prophets have spoken! Was it not necessary for the Christ** (Messiah) **to suffer these things and to enter into His glory?**

Then Luke made an amazing assertion:

> **And beginning with Moses and with all of the Prophets, He explained to them the things concerning Himself in all the Scriptures.**

Jesus claimed that He is the Messiah promised in the Old Testament, that His crucifixion was a necessity, and that He has the authority to forgive sin and impart eternal life to those who respond to Him in faith. The writers of the New Testament affirmed this claim and it has been the message of the Church for nearly two thousand years.

It is extremely important that this message be confirmable, because Jesus also said, **"I am the way, and the truth, and the life; no one comes to the Father but through Me"** (John 14:6). If this assertion is true, then each of our *eternal destinies* depend on our response to Him. If Jesus Christ's claims are true, then God has a *moral imperative* to give us a sure way to verify them!

The Bible's central message can be verified by examining the writings of Moses and the prophets that Jesus asserted were talking about Him. Remember, these documents were written hundreds of years before He was born. They were even translated from Hebrew to Greek about one hundred fifty years before His birth, and copies of that translation exist even to this day.

The astounding claim of Jesus is that these Old Testament documents, written hundreds of years before His birth, were talking specifically about Him. He claimed He was the Messiah promised in the writings of Moses and the prophets. These writings, by Moses and the prophets, became part of the Book of Books -- *The Bible*.

The Bible is like a two act play. The Old Testament (Act One) looks forward to God providing a Redeemer. It sets the stage for the second act when the Redeemer visits mankind, an event recorded in the New Testament. Both parts begin with history. But these records are not merely about mankind. They tell us that God, the Creator of the universe, has Himself acted in human history to meet mankind's greatest need -- spiritual redemption.

While the Bible has two major parts, and each part has many individual books, it is really one book. These books were written by many men who lived over a time span of more than a thousand years. But they have an amazing unity and synergism.

The Old Testament, the New Testament, and the individual books within each are all interdependent on one another. The themes in the New Testament are in the Old Testament, concealed, and those in the Old Testament are in the New Testament, revealed. When read exclusive of one another the Old Testament is a book without an ending, and the New Testament is a book without a beginning. Together they tell one story -- the story of man's rebellion and God's loving actions to make possible the redemption and restoration of fellowship with Himself.

The books of the Bible are like individual instruments in an orchestra. When combined, they produce a magnificent symphony. This book will help you appreciate the central *melody* (*plot*) in this symphony. As the writings of the many human authors blend together, the interrelationship of the Old and New Testament Scriptures will become clear. The New Testament is the fulfillment and thus an explanation of the Old. The Old Testament provides the *roots* for the New. From this synergism it is clear that the Maestro who conducted this symphony is the Lord God, Himself.

While this book will be of value if you are a believer who desires a better knowledge of the Bible's *big picture*, it will also be informative if you have doubts, and you want to examine the evidence to determine if the Bible's message is valid. This book, written by one who openly admits to being an advocate, summarizes evidence that confirms the personal claims of Jesus. *You owe it to yourself* to consider this evidence, and to render your personal verdict. Remember, your verdict may have eternal ramifications. As you read this book, you will also acquire a comprehension of the Bible's *big picture* that will stick with you for the rest of your life, and you will find some -- *GOOD NEWS!*

The
Master Plot
of the Bible

Robert L. Prall, M.Div.

Emmaus Books Trust
Houston, Texas

ISBN 0-9657835-0-2

Quantity prices are available
upon request by writing:

Emmaus Books
P. O. Box 73486
Houston, Texas 77273-3486

E-Mail addresses
Publisher - books@hisbride.org
Author - bobprall@yahoo.com

Emmaus Books Trust web page
www.hisbride.org/books.htm

Cover design by Randy Thompson
Artec, Houston, Texas

Table of Contents

INTRODUCTION

A few years after graduating from the University of Oregon, I committed my life to Christ, and about six months later I enrolled at Western Conservative Baptist Theological Seminary in Portland, Oregon. As a new believer with little Bible background, seminary was at first an overwhelming experience. Many of my fellow students had a lifetime of Bible study, and some were graduates of Christian colleges where they had taken courses on the Bible. I had a lot of catching up to do!

I knew I needed to get a grasp on the overall plot of the Bible so I could understand the individual parts. I found most sermons, books, and teachings used an analytical approach that dealt with selected topics in depth. That method was like studying with a microscope. I knew that I needed a view of the Bible using wide-angle binoculars. As a new believer, I needed a foundation from a synthetic study -- an overview.

One of my seminary professors suggested several books to help me comprehend the Bible's big picture. So, I devoted the summer vacation following my first year in seminary to studying these books and developing an understanding of how the parts of the Bible fit together and relate to one another. That was the beginning of my preparation to write this book.

After graduating from theological seminary, I joined the staff of Campus Crusade for Christ. This was in the mid-sixties, and we held summer Leadership Training Institutes (LTI's) for college students at Arrowhead Springs, in San Bernardino, California. At these conferences, we had a main speaker and several one-hour seminars taught by various staff members. One of the seminar topics was "Bible Overview."

As a seminary graduate, I was asked to teach the "Bible Overview" seminar at several of those training institutes. Since I only had an hour to work with, I suggested that the students keep their Bibles closed for the hour, and I would talk them through the plot of the Bible. I do not know how much the students retained, because I had to move awfully fast to cover the whole Bible in one hour. But, the preparation for those seminars, deciding just what to include and how to explain the unity of the biblical plot, and then repeatedly teaching the seminar, was an extremely valuable experience for me.

Teaching those "Bible Overview" seminars at the LTI's turned out to be the beginning of a lifelong ministry of helping others understand the overall flow of the Bible's message. I later expanded the seminar for use as a series of messages for student retreats. Then later, as the pastor of Grace Bible Church in College Station, Texas, I further expanded the messages and taught them as a series of Sunday morning messages spread out over a spring semester.

When I left the pastorate, I started teaching the same material for home Bible studies, student groups (mostly at Texas A&M University), and churches. As I taught this study, one group led to another, and the more I taught it, the more I enjoyed teaching it. I found that people were growing in their faith and getting excited about the Bible. Many who attended the classes later shared with me that the classes had given them a foundation for understanding the Bible they had been lacking. I finally came to realize that this study was the primary way I was to exercise my teaching gift.

I have found that many believers have studied individual parts of the Bible, but do not have a handle on the big picture. Or, put another way, they have studied a tree here, and a tree there, but have never seen a picture of the forest. Other than some of the Old Testament stories, and the books of Psalms and Proverbs, most of the *trees* they have studied are in the New Testament. My calling seems to be to help people get a clear picture of the forest. I am dedicated to helping people understand the interrelationship of the Old and New Testaments and how it all fits together as a unified whole. It is my conviction that without an understanding of the Old Testament "roots," one's understanding of the New Testament is limited.

For years, my notes for these messages were primarily in my head and the margins of my Bible. Finally, I decided I should also put the content into a more complete written form, thus this book. The objective of this book is not to give an exhaustive knowledge of the content of the Bible, rather to give the readers a basic *understanding* of the Bible's message that will stick with them for the rest of their lives and prepare them for a lifetime of further study.

To accomplish this objective, this book concentrates on foundational and transitional passages in the Bible. At times it gives extra attention to passages that are particularly significant, or ones that have been very meaningful in my own life.

As the Bible's plot is developed, at times it will be like putting together a picture puzzle. During the early phases of putting the borders together on a jigsaw puzzle, it is hard to see what the picture will be. As sections of a puzzle start to fit together, you begin to get an idea of what it will look like, and finally a perspective of the picture becomes clear. As you proceed with the puzzle, it becomes easier and easier to fit individual pieces into the big picture. So also, in this book, some *borders* will have to be set in place. It may seem at times as if we are detouring from the main plot, but as we proceed to put the pieces together, the unity of the whole biblical message will become clear, and you will see that these detours contain important foundational truths that are vital elements to comprehend the complete message.

This book includes extensive passages from the Bible. Rather than sending the readers to the Bible to look up texts, they are all included in this book. So that the readers can differentiate between biblical texts and my comments, the passages from the Bible are in **bold print.** To understand the message in this book, *you need to read these passages; because quite often this book lets the passages in the Scriptures speak for themselves without editorial comments.*

Furthermore, the Scripture passages are much more important than anything I (the author) have to say, so do not skip over them, even if they are passages you have read many times in the past. In most cases the verse numbers are eliminated, and the text is put in paragraph form for ease of reading. (The division of the Bible's books into chapters and verses was not part of the original texts. They were added centuries later to help people find particular passages more easily).

Because there are many who have greatly contributed to my Bible knowledge, it is only appropriate that I acknowledge certain people who have impacted my ministry. First there is Bob Luther, the pastor who led me to Christ when he was in his first pastorate in Aumsville, Oregon. Bob was also a fellow seminarian (I sort of pushed him through seminary as he was not about to let his "Timothy" graduate ahead of him). At Western Baptist Seminary in Portland, I had three professors who made particular impacts on my life: Dr. Arthur Whiting, Dr. Fred Howe, and Dr. Earl Radmacher. During my years with Campus Crusade, Dr. Bill Bright, the founder of Campus Crusade for Christ, and fellow staff member, Jon Braun, made important contributions to my understanding of the Bible. If you look closely, you will find the fingerprints of all of these men on the pages of this book!

I would also like to express my appreciation to Keith Gilmore, whom I don't know well, but who originated the "Walk Through the Bible" teaching technique using pantomime. I went through a series of classes Keith taught and appreciated his encouragement to use what the Lord had given him. When I added his "Walk Through" to the content I had been teaching, it greatly improved my presentation of the material. This encouraged me to keep teaching it, and ultimately lead to my writing this book.

I would also like to thank my wife, Jane, for her moral support and prayer as I wrote this book. I am also grateful to several friends at Northwest Bible Church in Houston, who proofread the manuscript, made suggestions, and helped me improve my writing skills.

Finally, one of my motivations to write this book was my son, Rob, informing me that I was going to be a grandfather. When I thought about having grandchildren, I concluded that by the time they would be old enough to go through my teaching series, I might be long gone! So I set out to put the Bible study series, I had taught many times, into book form for their benefit. My first grandchild, Kylie Noel Prall was born shortly before this book went to print. I hope to have more grandchildren, and this book is dedicated to all of them.

Whether you want to expand your Bible knowledge, or have doubts and questions about the validity of the Gospel, join with me in an adventure, and examine what I call *The Master Plot of the Bible.*

Chapter 1

Did God Really Say That?

Some years ago, one of my seminary professors, Dr. Earl Radmacher, was speaking on a college campus. A student came up to him after he ended his lecture and, using the "hippie" jargon of that day, suggested they go to a coffee shop so they could "rap" about his lecture. As they chatted over coffee, Earl quoted a Bible verse and explained it. The student said, "Well, I don't see it that way. That's just your interpretation of the Bible. I interpret it differently, and my interpretation is just as good as any other!" Earl responded by asking, "Where is the paper?" The student said, "What do you mean, where is the paper?" Earl responded, "You said we were going to come here to *rap*, so where is the wrapping paper so we can *wrap*?" The student responded, "That's not what I meant!" To which Earl chuckled and said, "Hey! My interpretation of what you said is just as good as any other!"

Is one interpretation just as good as any other? If the Bible is merely a book written by a group of men who were expressing their personal opinions, then the opinions of others might have equal value in one's search for meaning and purpose. But, the Bible claims to be much more than the assorted opinions of a group of men. *It claims to be a message from God to the human race.* This brings up two preliminary questions we will look at before we examine the plot of the Bible. First, "Where did the Bible come from?" and second, the issue from the above illustration, "How should it be interpreted?"

Where Did the Bible Come From?

The Bible claims to be a revelation from God. It says, **"All Scripture is inspired by God and profitable for teaching, for reproof, for correction, for training in righteousness;"** (II Timothy 3:16) and **"For no prophecy was ever made by an act of human will, but men moved by the Holy Spirit spoke from God"** (II Peter 1:21). Many texts in the Old Testament claim to be the Lord speaking to or through the human author with sayings such as, **"The Lord said," "Thus says the Lord,"** and **"The word of the Lord came to me."** The Apostle Paul clearly claimed the message he presented in the New Testament was not something he made up, rather a revelation from Jesus Christ. **"For I would have you know brethren, that the gospel which was preached by me is not according to man. For I neither received it from man, nor was I taught it, but I received it through a revelation of Christ."** (Galatians 1:11-12). The clear claim of Scripture is that while humans wrote the Bible, the initiative for their writing it was an act of God.

The message of the Bible is presented in a historical context that explains why God took the initiative to reveal Himself to man. It tells us that God originally intended for man to have fellowship with Himself, but man rebelled and became estranged from God. So, God chose a particular family He could use to provide His Redeemer for the rebellious human race. That family became a nation, Israel, and God used men from that nation as His channels to communicate the message about His plan, and later His actions, to provide redemption.

God chose a family that became the nation of Israel, to be the medium He would use to provide His Redeemer for mankind. Then God used men from that nation as channels to communicate His message about redemption!

Notice, the Bible not only claims to be a revelation from God, it also tells us that *God has acted in history to accomplish something for mankind.* As we explore the biblical records, we will see it is vital that we understand *what* God has done to fulfill His plan of redemption. The way God chose to communicate and preserve this crucial information was by using selected men to give us a written revelation. But the entire revelation was not given through one writer. Rather, God chose to reveal His Word progressively, in the context of the flow of history. The finished product is what we now call the Bible.

The Bible tells us God has acted in history to accomplish something for mankind!

How Should the Bible be Interpreted?

Since the Bible claims to be a revelation from God, it is important that we properly understand the message it intends to communicate. This brings us to the question, "Did God really say that?'

The goal of one who endeavors to interpret the Bible should be to first discover the meaning intended by the original authors, and from that to determine what God's message is to us -- not to give biblical passages whatever meaning appeals to the interpreter. Interpretation of the Bible should not be an exercise in self-expression.

Interpretation of the Bible should not be an exercise in self-expression.

When one wants to communicate a message, one must first select a medium of communication. Take the message, "I love you!" It has been communicated through many mediums, including poetry, literature, art, and music. Each medium of communication has its own laws or principles.

Using music as an example, let's assume two men are going to interpret Bach. The two are Dave Brubeck (a great jazz musician) and Arturo Toscanini (a great symphony conductor). If Brubeck played Bach, what would we hear? Probably a little Bach, and a lot of Brubeck. Toscanini, on the other hand, had a rare gift. He could virtually *"hear the music"* as he read a full symphony score on paper. Consequently, because of this ability, Toscanini is known as one of the greatest interpreters of Bach who ever lived.

How we interpret the Bible is particularly important, for we have seen the Bible claims that **"All Scripture is God-breathed ..."** (II Timothy 3:16), and **"But first of all, that no prophecy of Scripture is a matter of one's own interpretation.** (II Peter 1:20). While we may enjoy giving someone like Brubeck freedom to express himself when playing the music of other human composers, we need to be careful that we do not alter the message when it is from the Lord God!

There is much debate over whether the Bible should be interpreted literally. In consideration of the many misconceptions associated with the term *literal,* I prefer to use a different term. I call it *natural interpretation*: that which comes naturally from the text when one is honestly trying to be "a Toscanini," rather than "a Brubeck."

Natural interpretation first asks, "What is the nature of the text?" In some cases, it is obvious that figurative language was intended. For example, Jesus did not mean to convey He was a plank of wood with hinges when He said, "I am the door." He was obviously using the word *door* as a metaphor for the idea: "a way to enter."

When figurative language is used, it must be determined what message the original author intended.

When figurative language is used, it must be determined what message the original author intended. In most cases, when one carefully examines the text and considers the context, the intended message is clear. While there are many difficult passages in the Scriptures, and good men often differ in their interpretation, such passages rarely impact and never alter the central message of the Bible. *God gave us a clear revelation, not a guessing game!*

One of the most important factors in sound interpretation is to consider the context of passages. The classic illustration of someone who ignored the context is the young man who decided he was going to open his Bible randomly, point to a verse on the page, and follow its teaching that day. The first verse his finger fell on read, "... and Judas hanged himself." He decided the verse did not apply to him, so he flipped over a few pages and pointed to a second verse. It read, "Go and do thou likewise!"

Everyone understands the need to look at the immediate context, but it is also important to understand that passages have a broad context. Both the immediate and broad contexts should be considered when interpreting a text of the Scriptures. Sometimes, an understanding of the broad context can give one a comprehension of a passage that would be missed if it were not known. Other times, it can even change one's understanding of a message.

Both the immediate and the broad contexts must be considered when interpreting a text in the Bible.

The difference between the immediate and the broad context becomes clear when one considers the Book of Job, the oldest book in the Bible. This great classic deals with the age old question "Why do the righteous suffer?"

One could read a whole section of chapters in Job and conclude that Job suffered because he sinned. Then there is another section of chapters that seem to teach that Job's suffering was intended to teach him something, but because of Job's bad attitude he was not learning the intended lesson. But, when the context of the entire book is understood, it is obvious that both of these explanations were merely the opinions of some of Job's friends, and they were *not* the reason Job suffered. The broad context tells us that Job was going through a test that would not have been a valid test if he understood it.

When the broad context of Job is considered, Job teaches us many lessons. It teaches us that the misfortunes that we experience are not necessarily either consequences of our previous actions or a judgment from God. Job also teaches us that we should not jump to the conclusion that a sickness, serious injury, or other misfortune is punishment imposed upon us by God.

There is also a broad context that consists of the message of the whole Bible. The life, death, and resurrection of Jesus Christ, found in the New Testament, must be understood in the light of the setting and context established by the Old Testament. This book is designed to help its readers better understand the Old Testament *roots* for the New Testament message and thus better understand the Bible's broad context. I call this broad context -- *"The Master Plot of the Bible."*

Do you mean to tell me the Bible has a central PLOT?

A common response to the title of this book is: "What do you mean by the *plot* of the Bible?" Webster has several definitions for the word *plot*, including "the plan or main story of a literary work" and "a secret plan for accomplishing an (often evil or unlawful) end." As we proceed through the Bible, we will see its *plot* is not secret, evil, or unlawful, but it is more than just "the main plan or story of a literary work." The Bible's plot definitely includes the concept of: *"an intelligently planned course of action designed to accomplish an end or purpose."*

While the human authors of the Bible were unaware that their writings were going to become part of a larger book with a central plot, God chose to progressively reveal His plan through the writings of men whom He selected and inspired. The result is a "Book of Books" written by many men from several centuries. This book of many books has an amazing unity, and one central *plot* that begins in Genesis, and flows through the Bible to the book of the Revelation.

To prepare you for the rest of this book, the foundation for the Bible's plot rests on certain covenants and prophetic promises that God made in the Old Testament, which provide the basis for His actions on our behalf -- actions recorded in the New Testament. Understanding these promises, and God's work to fulfill them, helps us understand the Bible's plot. When the plot is understood, the individual parts of the Bible, that rest on the primary message, become much more meaningful.

Like the opening of a rose bud, the Bible's plot unfolds gradually. When the full bloom viewed, it is a magnificent creation. It is because of this gradual development, within a very long book, that the *plot* is often missed by many readers. In this book, we will skip over much of the material that rests on the main plot, not because it is unimportant, but to help you, the reader, grasp the main flow of biblical truth. Then you will be prepared to joyfully appreciate the many *"buds"* that spring off of the *"main stem."* Please be patient as we begin -- *the flower will gradually reach full bloom.*

Chapter 2
The Story Line

Do not feel alone if you have tried to read the Bible from cover to cover, and you got bogged down in the details someplace between the end of Genesis and the beginning of Deuteronomy. If this has been your experience, you need to know that is a common story. For some it's a chapter of "who begot whom" that it is the stopper; for others it's the details for the construction of the tabernacle, and for others it is the length (it is very long). It is not uncommon for readers to feel as if they have hit a solid brick wall when they try to read through the Bible.

The context of God's revelation to man is historical. Both the Old Testament and the New Testament begin with history. While one does not need to know the history in great detail to understand the plot, a general understanding of the historical flow is needed to comprehend the foundational and transitional passages in their contexts. So, like beginning on a jigsaw puzzle, this chapter will put some historical *borders* in place so we can, in later chapters, place pieces in the big picture.

In an abbreviated form, the following historical sketch contains most of the main events of the Bible. These events give us a context for God's revelation of redemption for mankind. In this book, this sequence of events is called "The Story Line". But, the story is not the *plot*. The *plot* will be examined when we dig into what God is doing within this story in future chapters.

The Bible tells us that the human race was created in God's image and after His likeness. Exercising his free will, man rebelled and broke fellowship with God. As a result of this rebellion, man's nature changed and the human race became sinful. Immediately thereafter, God promised He would take the initiative to provide redemption. The Bible is the unfolding of this "drama of redemption."

After recording some of man's early failures, the main story of redemption begins in Genesis twelve with four people: Abram (later renamed Abraham), his wife Sarai (later renamed Sarah), his father Terah, and his nephew Lot. The family was living in Ur of the Chaldeans, a city on the Euphrates River. God told Abram to leave Ur, take his clan, and move to the land of Canaan. They stopped at Haran on their way. At Haran, Abram's father Terah died, and God made a covenant with Abram. At the time, Abram was seventy-five years old.

Following God's instructions, Abram and his family moved on to the land of Canaan. In Canaan, Abram had two sons, Ishmael and Isaac. Isaac also had two sons, Jacob and Esau. Jacob, who was later renamed Israel, had twelve sons and one daughter, named Dinah.

Adam   Abraham   Isaac   Jacob (re-named Israel)   12 sons
——►

The descendants of the twelve sons of Jacob (Israel) are referred to in the Bible as Hebrews, the twelve tribes of Israel, the Jews (originally referring to descendants of Judah -- later applied to the whole nation), the children of Israel, the sons of Israel, or just Israel. Actually, there were thirteen tribes. One son, named Joseph, had two sons, Ephraim and Manasseh, who each became the fountainhead of a tribe. The Levites (descendants of a son named Levi) were the priestly tribe, and were not counted as one of the twelve. Though it's not exactly correct, for ease of remembering it is often said that each of the twelve sons of Israel became one of the twelve tribes of Israel.

Abraham's grandson, Jacob, had twelve sons. The descendants of these sons became twelve tribes of Israel.

The youngest of the twelve sons was Benjamin. The second youngest was Joseph. Joseph was a dreamer and had a coat of many colors, and the older ten brothers were jealous of him. So, they took Joseph, put him in a hole in the ground, then sold him to some descendants of Ishmael who were passing through on their way to Egypt. The Ishmaelites took Joseph to Egypt where they sold him as a slave.

Joseph's first stop in Egypt was the house of a rich Egyptian named Potiphar. As a servant in Potiphar's house, Joseph rejected advances from Potiphar's wife. She retaliated by making false claims against Joseph, and he ended up in prison. While in prison, Joseph interpreted some dreams and told of a coming famine. As a result, Joseph was released from jail, promoted, and became the number two man in all of Egypt -- second only to the Pharaoh (the title for their ruler).

When the famine came, the children of Israel, back in the land of Canaan, got hungry. So they sent representatives to Egypt to buy some food. When they arrived, Joseph recognized them (they did not recognize him); he sent them back and had them bring the whole clan to Egypt. The children of Israel spent about four hundred and thirty years in Egypt. They had thirty good years, then **"there arose a Pharaoh who knew not Joseph"** (Exodus 1:8 KJV), and they spent four hundred years under the whip of slavery.

God used Moses to deliver the children of Israel from bondage in Egypt, and through Moses, He gave them the law.

At the end of the four hundred and thirty years, God raised up a deliverer named Moses. Moses said to Pharaoh, **"Let my people go!"** (Exodus 5:1 KJV). But, Pharaoh responded, "No!" So God used Moses to deliver ten plagues on Egypt, the final one being a judgment on Egypt that the Jewish people still commemorate by observing the Feast of Passover. Finally, as a result of the Passover, Pharaoh let the children of Israel go. They left Egypt, passed through the Red Sea, and took a right turn to Mount Sinai. At Mount Sinai, through Moses, God gave the children of Israel two things -- the Law and the pattern for the Tabernacle (technically, a part of the Law).

When the Israelites came out from Mount Sinai, God had them count the people. That is the source for the name for the Old Testament book of Numbers. They then came to a town called Kadesh Barnea. At Kadesh Barnea, they sent twelve spies into the land, but they returned with two opinions. The majority report, from ten spies, warned them that there were giants in the land, and that they were like grasshoppers beside them. The minority report from two spies, Joshua and Caleb, said, the Lord is with us. Let's take the land! (Numbers 13, a paraphrase).

As a result of following the majority, the children of Israel spent forty years wandering around in the wilderness. At the end of the forty years, they counted the people again. Then Moses gave five messages, which became the Book of Deuteronomy, the book of reviews -- also referred to as the second giving of the Law.

Moses died before the children of Israel entered into the Promised Land. After his death, Joshua led the people through the Jordan River (from the East) and into the land. The first town they came to was Jericho. After marching around the city, **"the walls came tumbling down"** (Joshua 6:20 KJV). The second town was Ai, where they had some problems because of a member of the clan named Achan. After finally experiencing a victory at Ai, they conquered the land to the south. Then they turned north, and conquered the land to the north.

After victories in the north and the south, they divided the land, with each tribe getting a portion. The tribes of Gad, half of Mannaseh, and Reuben took their portions on the east side of the Jordan river. The rest settled on the west side.

In those days, Israel did not have a king, and the people went through ups and downs recorded in the book of Judges. The children of Israel would repeatedly chase after one of the heathen gods and end up in bondage; then God would raise up a judge to deliver them. Then they would begin the cycle again. The book of Judges explains why they went through these cycles when it records, **"In those days, there was no king in Israel; every man what was right in his own eyes."** (NASB - A verse repeated many times in the book of Judges.)

The last of the judges and the first of the prophets was Samuel. When Samuel was about to die, the children of Israel did not want Samuel's sons as judges, so they said, **"We want to be like all of the people around us. We want a king!"** (I Samuel chapter eight - paraphrase). After warning them of the negatives a king would impose on them, they still insisted they wanted one, so God consented and gave them a king.

FROM EGYPT   TO THE WILDERNESS   INTO THE LAND   JUDGES   KINGS

The first king was Saul. He was the king who had the crown removed from him. The second was David. He was the great conquering king. The third king was Solomon. He was famous because of his wisdom and wives. No one seems to understand how he got that combination.

When Solomon died, his son Rehoboam became king. After a big debate, Rehoboam raised the taxes, and it caused a revolt. So, a leader named Jeroboam led the ten northern tribes in splitting off from the southern tribes. Consequently, there were then two kingdoms.

The southern kingdom was called Judah, and the northern kingdom was called Israel. The dominant tribe in the southern kingdom was Judah. Benjamin and the Levites also remained in the southern kingdom. The dominant tribe in the northern kingdom was Ephraim. It included Ephraim and the remaining nine tribes. At times when the Bible speaks of "Judah," it is speaking of the whole southern kingdom, and at times when it speaks of "Ephraim," it is a reference to all ten tribes in the northern kingdom.

SAUL DAVID SOLOMON REHOBOAM   SOUTHERN KINGDOM (JUDAH)

JEROBOAM NORTHERN KINGDOM (ISRAEL)

After the kingdom was divided, the successive kings in the North were all bad. The kings in the South were mostly bad, but they had four good kings, and three who were "so so." In 721 B.C., the Assyrians conquered the ten northern tribes and took them off to Assyria. They are now referred to as "the ten lost tribes of Israel." Later, in 586 B.C., Nebuchadnezzar, King of Babylon, conquered the southern kingdom and took them as captives to Babylon.

The people in the southern kingdom remained in captivity at Babylon for about seventy years and were allowed to return to Jerusalem at the time of Zerrubbabel, Ezra, and Nehemiah. When they returned, the first order of business was to rebuild the temple. Then they rebuilt the wall around Jerusalem. The Old Testament ends, and there were four hundred years of silence (no biblical revelation) until the birth of Jesus. (Note: The Roman Catholic Bible includes some books, called the Apocryhpha, during that time span.)

Southern Kingdom   Babylonian Captivity   Returned to the Land
——▶

Northern Kingdom to Assyria (Ten Lost Tribes)
——▶

The Drama is Resumed -- The New Testament

The New Testament begins with the four Gospel accounts of the birth, life, ministry, crucifixion, and resurrection of Jesus Christ. The book of Acts tells of the ascension of Jesus Christ, the pouring out of the Holy Spirit, the establishment of the Church, and the spread of the Gospel from **"Jerusalem, and in all Judea and Samaria, and even to the remotest part of the earth"** (Acts 1:8).

The first part of Acts is centered in Jerusalem with the central character being Peter. The remaining part of Acts focuses on the Apostle Paul and his missionary journeys.

Earthly ministry of Christ Crucifixion, Resurrection, & Ascension
——▶

The Gospel from Jerusalem, to Judea, to Samaria, and to the world
——▶

The primary historical framework can be found in just eleven of the thirty-nine books in the Old Testament, and in two of the twenty-seven books in the New Testament. While other books provide more history, their messages relate to what was happening within the time periods covered by these thirteen books.

It is also helpful to understand that the books of the Bible are not organized sequentially. Rather, they are grouped according to their content. The charts on the next page show the time relationships between the respective books.

The left hand column on the first chart lists the eleven books that provide the framework for the Old Testament and shows where the rest of the books in the Old Testament fit within the time context of these eleven.

OLD TESTAMENT	(Book names in bold type)	
1	**Genesis**	From the creation of the earth to Joseph in Egypt.
		Job
2	**Exodus**	From Moses through Mount Sinai.
		Leviticus
3	**Numbers**	Starts and ends with the people being counted.
		Deuteronomy
4	**Joshua**	Entering the land, conquering, and dividing it
5	**Judges**	The ups and downs under the rule of the Judges.
		Ruth
6	**I Samuel**	The book of King Saul.
7	**II Samuel**	The book of King David.
		I Chronicles Psalms
8	**I Kings**	The book of King Solomon.
		II Chronicles (Part in context of II Kings)
		Proverbs Ecclesiastes Song of Solomon
9	**II Kings**	The divided kingdom, taken to Assyria & Babylon.
	Pre-Exile Prophets	**Isaiah, Jeremiah, Lamentations, Hosea, Joel, Amos Amos, Jonah, Micah, Nahum, Habakkuk & Zephaniah**
		There is no historical book for the time of the Babylonian captivity, though some history of that period is learned from the Exilic prophets:
	Exilic Prophets	**Ezekiel, Daniel,** and **Obadiah** (Obadiah may have been pre-exile).
10	**Ezra**	*After their captivity in Babylon, the children of Israel*
11	**Nehemiah**	*returned to the land to rebuild Jerusalem & the temple*
		Esther
	Post-Exilic Prophets:	

NEW TESTAMENT	(Book names in bold type)	
12	**Matthew**	The main historical flow of the life of Jesus Christ.
	Mark	
	Luke	*The other Gospels record the same historical ministry of Jesus, but each from a somewhat different perspective.*
	John	
13	**Acts**	The spread of the Gospel and formation of the Church.
	The Christian Church Epistles - Letters written to local churches.	
		Romans, I & II Corinthians, Galatians, Ephesians, Philippians, Colossians, I & II Thessalonians - written to individuals who were pastors.
	The Pastoral Epistles - Letters written to individuals who were pastors	
		I & II Timothy, Titus, Philemon
	The Hebrew Christian Epistles - Letters to Hebrew believers	
		Hebrews, James, I & II Peter, I, II, & III John, Jude
	The Final Book of the Bible - An epilogue that looks to the future.	
		The Revelation

The main historical framework for the New Testament is in two books, **Matthew** and **Acts**. Additional history is learned in other books, but these two provide the historical flow of events.

The other historical books either tell some of the same history from different perspectives, or tell of events or teachings that are not necessary to follow the story line. When one understands that the books of the Bible do not follow one another chronologically, it helps when digging into the messages of individual books of the Bible.

God gave us His progressive revelation in the context of history

---

For example, Jeremiah is known as the Weeping Prophet. When he wrote the book of Lamentations, Jeremiah was *lamenting* that the children of Israel were about to be taken captive to Babylon. To fully understand Lamentations, the corresponding historical passages in II Kings (or II Chronicles) should be read first.

The same thing is true of other biblical books and passages. Though their placement in the Bible may not be right next to each other (there are in our example a dozen books between II Kings and Lamentations), each book fits into the overall historical framework and needs to be understood in its historical setting. Hopefully, the above charts will be helpful as you study the Bible.

It should be noted, the version of the Old Testament used by the Protestants has the same books as the one used by the Jewish people, but they are arranged in a different order. The differing order does not change the message. The Old Testament used by Roman Catholics includes some books not included in either the Jewish or Protestant versions, but these extra books do not alter the Bible's plot. The books are the same in the New Testament translations used by Protestants and Roman Catholics.

Always remember, God gave us His progressive revelation in the context of history. The Bible is not a book on philosophy. It is a historical revelation from God. Both the Old and New Testaments begin with historical sections. The stories of the Bible are all part of history. While the Bible records events from human history, it also reveals that God is active in that history, working to accomplish His ultimate purposes.

The biblical records reveal that God is active in history, working to accomplish His ultimate purposes.

Within the context of biblical history, there is a master plot that begins in Genesis and carries through to the book of the Revelation. It is the most important plot any person can understand. *The Bible's plot not only tells us what God has done in the past, but it also tells us what God is now doing for us, and what He will do in the future to complete our redemption.* We will begin our survey of the plot in the following chapter.

This story line for the Bible's history is given to help you grasp the historical context of the plot. It may be helpful to review it several times.

SUMMARY OF CHAPTER TWO:

God has chosen to reveal Himself to us in a historical setting. The Bible's plot is given in the context of this history, and it tells us what God has done, is now doing, and will do in the future to fulfill His purpose for our being here on earth. It is helpful for one to develop an understanding of the flow of the main historical events in the Bible so the *plot* can be more fully comprehended. (The main *story line* of that history is given in this chapter for that purpose, and it may be a good idea to review it several times.)

While there are a total of sixty-six books in the Bible, the main historical flow can be traced in thirteen books, eleven in the Old Testament and two in the New Testament. While there are other books that are historical, they either cover some of the same history from a different perspective or fall within the context of the thirteen main historical books. The books of the Bible are organized by type of content and are not always in chronological order.

Chapter 3
In the Beginning - The Promise

"In the beginning God created the heaven and the earth. ... And the Lord God formed man of the dust of the ground, and breathed into his nostrils the breath of life" (Genesis 1:1 & 2:7 KJV). Genesis, chapters one and two, tell us that God created the universe, and He created man. Apparently, God created the human race so men and women could have fellowship with Him. Genesis, chapters two and three, record that man was created in God's image and after His likeness. But, as an act of his free will, man rebelled against God and, as a result, man died spiritually. This spiritual death produced in man a sinful nature, and thus man broke fellowship with God.

Romans 5:12 explains the long term consequences: "Therefore, just as through one man sin entered into the world, and death through sin, and so death spread to all men, because all sinned ...." Just as a father passes on a genetic defect to his children, the first man's sinful nature has been passed on to all in the human race. But, immediately after the fall, God promised that He would eventually send someone who would provide victory and redemption (the seed of the woman). (Genesis 3:14-15). The rest of the Bible records the outworking of God's promise.

While the story of the fall of man tells how mankind became sinful, it also gives us hope. If one denies the Bible's record of the fall, then it logically follows that we are, in our present sinful condition, as God intended us to be. That would be bad news. Or, if one adopts the evolutionary hypothesis, that man just happened by chance and the only hope for our improvement is in the "survival of the fittest," then Hitler's horrible solution of helping the process along by "eliminating the undesirables" follows as a logical conclusion. That would be even worse news.

Genesis three tells us man's sinful nature is not the nature originally given by God, thus there is hope for a *healing*. That is good news! When I taught a Bible study for a meeting of the Christian Veterinarian Society at the Veterinarian Medicine School at Texas A&M University, I explained it to them in a way they would understand. I told them, "It's hard to heal a well dog -- one that is in its natural condition! It is only the sick dog, one not in its natural condition, that can be healed." So also with man. Because man is spiritually *sick*, there is hope for healing. As we study the Bible's plot, we will look at what God has done, is now doing, and will do in the future to accomplish a spiritual healing for fallen men and women.

Genesis three tells us man's sinful nature is not the nature originally given by God, so there is hope for a "healing."

God Made a Covenant With Abram

After the record of the creation, the next few chapters in Genesis record some of man's early failures. Then, beginning in Genesis chapter twelve, and in some following chapters, God made a covenant with Abram (who was later renamed Abraham) and reiterated it to Abraham's son Isaac and his grandson Jacob. It is called the Abrahamic Covenant. (Some people refer to it as the Abrahamic Contract.) *An understanding of the Abrahamic Covenant is crucial to understanding the Bible's plot, because it lays the foundation for the rest of the Bible. Read these passages carefully:*

The Lord had said to Abram, "Leave your country, your people and your father's household and go to the land I will show you. I will make you into a great nation and I will bless you; I will make your name great, and you will be a blessing. I will bless those who bless you, and whoever curses you I will curse; and all peoples on earth will be blessed through you." So Abram left, as the Lord had told him; and Lot went with him. Abram was seventy-five years old when he set out from Haran ... and they set out for the land of Canaan, and they arrived there .... The Lord appeared to Abram and said, "To your offspring I will give this land." (Genesis 12:4-7)

The Lord said to Abram after Lot had parted from him, "Lift up your eyes from where you are and look north and south, east and west. All the land that you see I will give to you and your offspring forever. I will make your offspring like the dust of the earth, so that if anyone could count the dust, then your offspring could be counted. Go, walk through the length and breadth of the land, for I am giving it to you." (Genesis 13:14-17)

After this, the word of the Lord came to Abram in a vision: "Do not be afraid, Abram. I am your shield, your very great reward." But Abram said, "O Sovereign Lord, what can you give me since I remain childless and the one who will inherit my estate is Eliezer of Damascus?" And Abram said, "You have given me no children; so a servant in my household will be my heir." Then the word of the Lord came to him: "This man will not be your heir, but a son coming from your own body will be your heir." He took him outside and said, "Look up at the heavens and count the stars -- if indeed you can count them." Then he said to him, "So shall your offspring be." Abram believed the Lord, and he credited it to him as righteousness. He also said to him, "I am the Lord, who brought you out of Ur of the Chaldeans to give you this land to take possession of it." But Abram said, "O Sovereign Lord, how can I know that I will gain possession of it?" (Genesis 15:1-8)

On that day the Lord made a covenant with Abram and said, "To your descendants I give this land, from the river of Egypt to the great river, the Euphrates...." (Genesis 15:18)

When Abram was ninety-nine years old, the Lord appeared to him and said, "I am God Almighty; walk before me and be blameless. I will confirm my covenant between Me and you and will greatly increase your numbers." Abram fell face down, and God said to him, "As for me, this is my covenant with you: You will be the father of many nations. No longer will you be called Abram; your name will be Abraham, for I have made you a father of many nations. I will make you very fruitful; I will make nations of you, and kings will come from you. I will establish my covenant as an everlasting covenant between me and you and your descendants after you for the generations to come, to be your God and the God of your descendants after you. The whole land of Canaan, where you are now an alien, I will give as an everlasting possession to you and your descendants after you; and I will be their God." (Genesis 17:1-8)

God also said to Abraham, "As for Sarai your wife, you are no longer to call her Sarai; her name will be Sarah. I will bless her and will surely give you a son by her. I will bless her so that she will be the mother of nations; kings of peoples will come from her." Abraham fell face down; he laughed and said to himself, "Will a son be born to a man a hundred years old? Will Sarah bear a child at the age of ninety?" And Abraham said to God, "If only Ishmael might live under your blessing!" Then God said, "Yes, but your wife Sarah will bear you a son, and you will call him Isaac. I will establish my covenant with him as an everlasting covenant for his descendants after him. And as for Ishmael, I have heard you: I will surely bless him; I will make him fruitful and will greatly increase his numbers. He will be the father of twelve rulers, and I will make him into a great nation. But my covenant I will establish with Isaac, whom Sarah will bear to you by this time next year." (Genesis 17:15-21)

"I swear by myself," declares the Lord, "that because you have done this and have not withheld your son, your only son, I will surely bless you and make your descendants as numerous as the stars in the sky and as the sand on the seashore. Your descendants will take possession of the cities of their enemies, and through your offspring all nations on earth will be blessed, because you have obeyed me." (Genesis 22:16-18)

Later to Abraham's son Isaac, God said:

"Stay in this land for a while, and I will be with you and will bless you. For to you and your descendants I will give all these lands and will confirm the oath I swore to your father Abraham. I will make your descendants as numerous as the stars in the sky and will give them all these lands, and through your offspring all nations on earth will be blessed, because Abraham obeyed me and kept my requirements, my commands, my decrees and my laws" (Genesis 26:3 & 5)

Still later to Isaac's son Jacob (who was renamed Israel), God said:

There above it stood the Lord, and he said: "I am the Lord, the God of your father Abraham and the God of Isaac. I will give you and your descendants the land on which you are lying. Your descendants will be like the dust of the earth, and you will spread out to the west and to the east, to the north and to the south. All peoples on earth will be blessed through you and your offspring." (Genesis 28:13-14)

God's Promise to Abraham, Isaac, and Jacob

God promised three things in the Abrahamic Covenant, the *contract* He entered into with Abraham and affirmed to Isaac and Jacob:

1. **Land** - All the way from the river of Egypt to the Euphrates river. A lot of land, and it's land that has great political significance in our world today.

2. **Seed** - Descendants so numerous that if one tried to count them it would be like trying to count the stars in the sky, the dust of the earth, or the sand at the seashore -- so numerous they can not be counted.

3. **Blessings** - That all families would be blessed through Abraham. God did not tell Abraham how, or when, He would provide the blessings. He merely told him, I am going to make you a great nation, I will bless you, and through your descendants others from every nation in the world will be blessed!

It's important to understand that everything in the rest of the Bible relates back, at least indirectly, to the promise to Abraham of <u>land</u>, <u>seed</u>, and <u>blessings</u>. This is crucial for one to properly understand the Bible's message. The Bible is a progressive revelation and the rest of the Bible tells about the outworking of this covenant that God made with Abraham.

Everything in the rest of the Bible relates, at least indirectly, to the promise to Abraham of LAND, SEED, and BLESSINGS.

The texts that record the Abrahamic Covenant reiterate, several times, that the Abrahamic Covenant is an eternal covenant. That's very important. It was not merely given to Abraham, ceasing to exist after Abraham died. Rather, the Abrahamic Covenant is an eternal covenant. It was first given to Abraham, repeated to Isaac and Jacob, and continues on for the children of Israel, and the whole human race.

The importance of understanding the provisions of the Abrahamic Covenant cannot be over emphasized. They provide the foundation for the rest of the Bible's message of redemption. It could even be said: "If one does not understand the Abrahamic Covenant, one does not understand the message of the Bible, and one does not understand what is happening in history, or what is happening in the world -- even today."

The Abrahamic Covenant provides the foundation for the rest of the Bible's message of redemption.

If the importance of the Abrahamic Covenant is a new concept to you, let me suggest you backtrack three pages and again read the passages that give us this foundational truth. As you read these passages, notice that they include promises to Abraham individually; national promises for his descendants; and a universal promise for the whole human race.

Abrahamic Covenant: Conditional or Unconditional?

There is a very important question that needs to be answered before proceeding: "Is the Abrahamic covenant a conditional or an unconditional covenant?" The answer one gives to this question will have a major impact on how much of the rest of the Bible will be understood. If you see it as a conditional covenant, you will be led to one set of conclusions about God's plan for the future of the world. However, if you see it as an unconditional covenant, a different set of conclusions will logically flow from your answer to this question.

It is obvious that there were some initial commands given to Abraham. He obeyed some and disobeyed others (such as taking his family with him instead of leaving them). But, we read in Genesis fifteen: **"Abram believed the Lord, and he credited it to him as righteousness."** After fulfilling the condition of *faith*, Abraham asked God; **"O Sovereign Lord, how can I know that I will gain possession of it?"** (Genesis 15:8). Paraphrasing Abraham's response, he said, "I believe you God. But, how can I know for sure You will do Your part and fulfill Your promises?" God's answer to Abraham is of particular significance:

So the Lord said to him, "Bring me a heifer, a goat and a ram, each three years old, along with a dove and a young pigeon." Abram brought all these to him, cut them in two and arranged the halves opposite each other; the birds, however, he did not cut in half. Then birds of prey came down on the carcasses, but Abram drove them away. As the sun was setting, Abram fell into a deep sleep, and a thick and dreadful darkness came over him.

Then the Lord said to him, "Know for certain that your descendants will be strangers in a country not their own, and they will be enslaved and mistreated four hundred years."... When the sun had set and darkness had fallen, a smoking firepot with a blazing torch appeared and passed between the pieces. On that day the Lord made a covenant with Abram, saying, "To your descendants I have given this land, from the river of Egypt as far as the great river, the river Euphrates ...." (Genesis 15:9-18)

To understand God's answer, read a comment from Jeremiah:

"And I will give to the men who have transgressed My covenant, who have not fulfilled the words of the covenant which they made before Me, when they cut the calf in two and passed between its parts -- the officials of Judah, ... and all of the people of the land, who passed between the parts of the calf ..." (Jeremiah 34:18-19 NASB)

This passage was speaking about a later covenant made with the children of Israel. From it we learn that when two parties made a covenant (in their culture), the parties would take sacrifices, divide them in two parts and walk together between the pieces of the sacrifice. The symbolism is obvious. Both parties agreed to fulfill their part of the covenant.

In Genesis fifteen, when God made a covenant with Abraham, Abraham did not pass between the pieces of the sacrifices. The symbol of the Lord God passed between the pieces. Thus, God's dramatic answer to Abraham was that the fulfillment of His promise to Abraham is not dependent on what any other person does. It is solely dependent on what God does. In the New Testament book of Hebrews, there is a commentary that confirms that God's promise to Abraham became unconditional after Abraham fulfilled the initial condition when he responded in faith:

God's answer to Abraham was that the fulfillment of the promise rests solely on God's actions.

For when God made the promise to Abraham, since He could swear by no one greater, He swore by Himself, saying, "I will surely bless you, and I will surely multiply you." And thus having patiently waited, he obtained the promise. For men swear by one greater than themselves, and with them an oath given as confirmation is an end of every dispute. In the same way God, desiring even more to show to the heirs of the promise, the unchangeableness of His purpose, interposed with an oath (Hebrews 6:13-17).

Thus, the ultimate fulfillment of God's promises to Abraham is not dependent on anything that anyone beyond Abraham would do. After Abraham fulfilled his part of the covenant, the rest of the covenant is dependent only on the veracity of God's word and His ability to fulfill His part. Abraham fulfilled his part of the contract when he responded to God in faith: **"And he (Abram) believed in the Lord, and He (God) counted it to him for righteousness "** (Genesis 15:6 KJV). Only God's part of the contract was left to be fulfilled. Consequently, the Abrahamic Covenant became an unconditional covenant, or we could call it a *unilateral contract.*

God is fully capable of fulfilling His promises. No one can stop Him from accomplishing His purposes!

The book of Job tells us **"I know that You can do all things; and no plan of yours can thwarted."** (Job 42:2 KJV). Later in Job, God says this statement about Him is true! God is fully capable of fulfilling His promises, and no one can stop Him from accomplishing His purposes. His purpose will not change. From a human viewpoint, it may seem as if the world has no purpose. The Bible tells us otherwise. It not only has a purpose, but God is in full control, and He will make sure that His plan and purpose are accomplished. He announced His plan ahead of time in His covenant with Abraham. Since it is now an unconditional covenant, its fulfillment rests only upon the veracity of God's word and His ability to fulfill it.

Later in the Bible there are conditions given for *individuals* to participate in the benefits of the promise God gave to Abraham, but the ultimate fulfillment of the Abrahamic Covenant rests only on the veracity of God's word and His ability to fulfill it. God will finally fulfill every part of His contract with Abraham for:

Land
Seed
Blessings

SUMMARY OF CHAPTER THREE:

The foundation for everything in the rest of God's progressive revelation to mankind is found in the Abrahamic Covenant. In this covenant, God promised Abraham some **land** (from the river of Egypt to the Euphrates river); **seed** (descendants so numerous that they can not be counted); and **blessings** (for all families of the world).

While there were initial conditions given to Abraham, after he fulfilled those conditions, this covenant became unconditional. It was later confirmed to Abraham's son Isaac and his grandson Jacob (who was renamed Israel).

The New Testament book of Hebrews looks back to when God gave this covenant to Abraham, and it tells us that God's promise to Abraham is part of His purpose which will ultimately be accomplished.

The covenant promise God gave to Abraham laid a foundation. The rest of the Bible builds on this foundation and tells us how God will fulfill His promise to Abraham of land, seed, and blessings for all families of the earth.

CHAPTER 4
The Nature of Biblical Faith

Hebrews 11:6 tells us, **"And without faith it is impossible to please Him (God)."** For many, the concept of religious faith is a belief in something, even though there is no objective reason for believing it. Faith is often referred to as *blind faith*. This is not the Bible's concept of faith! The Bible uses illustrations from the life of Abraham to define biblical faith. Before we move on, we need to examine the nature of true biblical faith.

To explain faith, the New Testament looks at Abraham's faith when he believed God would fulfill His promise to give him a son through his wife Sarah. Sarah had been barren all of her life, and they were old enough to be great-grandparents when God promised them a son:

In hope against hope he (Abraham) believed in order that he might became the father of many nations, according to that which had been spoken, "So shall your offspring be." And without becoming weak in faith, he contemplated his own body, now as good as dead since he was about a hundred years old, and the deadness of Sarah's womb. Yet with respect to the promise of God, he did not waver in unbelief, but grew strong in faith, giving glory to God, and being fully assured that what He had promised, He was able also to perform. (Romans 4:18-21)

The New Testament also uses the event from Genesis twenty-two, when Abraham was tested at Mount Moriah, as an illustration of faith.

Then God said, "Take your son, your only son, Isaac, whom you love, and go to the region of Moriah. Sacrifice him there as a burnt offering on one of the mountains I will tell you about."

Early the next morning Abraham got up and saddled his donkey. He took with him two of his servants and his son Isaac. When he had cut enough wood for the burnt offering, he set out for the place God had told him about. On the third day Abraham looked up and saw the place in the distance. He said to his servants, "Stay here with the donkey while I and the boy go over there. We will worship and then we will come back to you."

Abraham took the wood for the burnt offering and placed it on his son Isaac, and he himself carried the fire and the knife. As the two of them went on together, Isaac spoke up and said to his father Abraham, "Father?" "Yes, my son?" Abraham replied. "The fire and wood are here," Isaac said, "but where is the lamb for the burnt offering?" Abraham answered, "God himself will provide the lamb for the burnt offering, my son." ...

When they reached the place God had told him about, Abraham built an altar there and arranged the wood on it. He bound his son Isaac and laid him on the altar, on top of the wood. Then he reached out his hand and took the knife to slay his son.

But the angel of the Lord called out to him from heaven, "Abraham! Abraham!" "Here I am," he replied. "Do not lay a hand on the boy," he said. "Do not do anything to him. Now I know that you fear God, because you have not withheld from me your son, your only son."

Abraham looked up and there in a thicket he saw a ram caught by its horns. He went over and took the ram and sacrificed it as a burnt offering instead of his son. So Abraham called that place "The Lord will provide." And to this day it is said, "On the mountain of the Lord it will be provided (Genesis 22:2-14).

The author of Hebrews comments on this event: **By faith Abraham, when he was tested, offered up Isaac, and he who had received the promises was offering up his only begotten son, it was to whom it was said, "In Isaac your seed will be called." He considered that God is able to raise men even from the dead..."** (Hebrews 11:17-19).

From these passages, and one to follow, we discover five factors of Abraham's faith. The first four are:

1. Abraham believed that God IS.
2. Abraham believed that God has made promises.
3. Abraham believed that God is able to fulfill His promises.
4. Abraham believed God will be faithful in fulfilling His promises.

Faith like Abraham's is not a fuzzy faith and is not a blind faith. It rests on the firm foundation of God's promises. *Biblical faith is our positive response to God's revealed promises.* The book of Hebrews tells us it should be a fixed faith; **"Fixing our eyes on Jesus, the author and perfecter of our faith, who for the joy set before Him endured the cross, despising the shame, and He sat down at the right hand of the throne of God."** (Hebrews 12:2)

Faith is a word that demands an object. It is like the word "throw." If someone says, "I throw," it is only natural to ask, "You throw WHAT?" If they answer, "I throw, throw," the natural response is: "That's ridiculous. You can not throw, throw; you have to throw something." A lot of people try to have faith in faith, and that is about like trying to throw, throw.

Faith is a word that demands a valid object

The word faith not only demands an object, but it is also important that the object is a valid object. The proper object of faith is God, His revealed promises, His ability to fulfill His promises, and His faithfulness in fulfilling His promises. It is not a blind leap of faith!

In Old Testament times, faith looked forward to what God would do to fulfill His promises. A New Testament believer's faith looks both backwards and forwards. It looks back to what God has done for us, and forward to the time when God will fulfill all of His promises. Another New Testament text, from the book of James, uses that event on Mount Moriah to teach us the fifth factor of faith;

What use is it my brethren, if a man says he has faith but has no works? Can that faith save him? ... But someone may will say, "You have faith and I have works; show me your faith without the works, and I will show you my faith by my works." You believe that God is one. You do well; the demons also believe and shudder. But are you willing to recognize, you foolish fellow, that faith without works is useless? Was not Abraham our father justified by works when he offered up Isaac his son on the altar? You see that faith was working with his works, and as a result of the works, faith was perfected. (James 2:14-23)

The fifth factor of Abraham's faith could be expressed:

5. Abraham's faith had "legs that walk."

If faith is genuine, it will result in action. A paraphrase of James could read, "If your faith does not have legs, it's a fraud!"

Real Faith has Legs that Walk

From one end of the Bible to the other, God tells us He loves us and wants to pour out His blessings on us. To receive His blessings, we must respond to Him in faith -- a faith validated by legs that walk!

Faith Without Works is Dead

It is very important that we understand the context of James' statement, **"faith without works is dead"** (James 2:17 KJV.) This verse is often misused because the context is ignored. In the illustration James used to establish this principle, the *good work* he cited was that Abraham *took action* as a result of *believing* what God had promised him. Abraham believed God when God told him he would have a son and that his son would have descendants who would be so numerous they could not be counted.

As we read above, in Hebrews 11:17-19, Abraham's belief that God would fulfill that promise was so strong that he was willing to follow God's instructions, even if it meant that God would have to perform a miracle (raising his son from the dead) to fulfill His promise. Abraham's faith walked consistently with his belief that God was able, and that He would be faithful in fulfilling His promise.

Biblical Faith Rests on God's Promises

Biblical faith is based on God's promises, but *not all promises in the Bible are for everyone.* There are many promises in the Bible that were for specific individuals and for Israel. We may be impacted by those promises, but we should not take them out of their context. Many believers have been disappointed because a biblical promise they *claimed for themselves* was not fulfilled. The problem in such cases is not with God's faithfulness, rather with faulty interpretation -- the promise was not given to them.

There are many promises directed to all who know Christ as Savior, and they may be properly claimed. God tells us what He has accomplished for us and what He will do in and through us, if we walk by faith -- a faith that focuses on God and His faithfulness.

Never divorce the fifth factor of faith (that real faith has legs that walk) from the first four factors: That God is, that He has made promises, that He is able to fulfill His promises, and that He is faithful in fulfilling His promises.

Good works do NOT produce a right relationship with God. They are the product of walking with Him.

We will see later in this book, that a walk in true biblical faith will naturally produce a life that is pleasing to God and man. Good deeds will always follow true faith. But remember, good works do not cause faith; rather, they are the effect -- a natural by-product of biblical faith. They are the natural result in the life of one who walks in true biblical faith -- a faith fixed on God's promises -- a faith so real that it has legs that walk.

Summary of Chapter Four:

Biblical faith is not a "fuzzy," subjective faith, it is not a blind faith, and it is not faith in faith. Faith is a word that demands an object, and the object of biblical faith is ultimately Jesus and His work for us on the cross. From the life of the Old Testament patriarch, Abraham, and the New Testament comments about his faith, we learn of five factors of faith. That God is. That He has made promises. That He is able to fulfill His promises. That He is faithful in fulfilling His promises. And, that real faith has legs that walk -- when someone walks in true biblical faith, it will have an impact in their life and actions.

CHAPTER 5
THE PROMISE IS Followed by THE LAW

After God made His covenant with Abraham, He gave Abraham a son named Isaac. Isaac then had two sons, Jacob and Esau. The Abrahamic Covenant was confirmed to both Isaac and Jacob. Jacob was renamed "Israel" and he had twelve sons. One of the sons, Joseph, was sold to slave traders and was taken to Egypt. In Egypt, Joseph was jailed for trumped up charges. While in jail, Joseph interpreted some dreams for the Pharaoh, told of a coming famine, and became a leader, second in command to Egypt's Pharaoh. As a result of the famine, the rest of the clan followed Joseph to Egypt. The children of Israel had thirty good years in Egypt; then they spent four hundred years as slaves of the Egyptians.

The Mosaic Covenant

After four hundred years in slavery, God raised up a deliverer named Moses. After God sent ten plagues, Pharaoh let the people go. They passed through the Red Sea and continued on to Mount Sinai. At Mount Sinai, God gave, through Moses, another covenant to the children of Israel. It was proposed to the Israelites and accepted by them in Exodus nineteen and is known as the Mosaic Covenant:

Then Moses went up to God, and the Lord called to him from the mountain and said, "This is what you are to say to the house of Jacob and what you are to tell the people of Israel: 'You yourselves have seen what I did to Egypt, and how I carried you on eagles' wings and brought you to myself. Now if

you obey me fully and keep my covenant, then out of all nations you will be my treasured possession. Although the whole earth is mine, you will be for me a kingdom of priests and a holy nation.' These are the words you are to speak to the Israelites."

So Moses went back and summoned the elders of the people and set before them all the words the Lord had commanded him to speak. The people all responded together, "We will do everything the Lord has said." So Moses brought their answer back to the Lord.

The Lord said to Moses, "I am going to come to you in a dense cloud, so that the people will hear me speaking with you and will always put their trust in you." Then Moses told the Lord what the people had said. And the Lord said to Moses, "Go to the people and consecrate them today and tomorrow. Have them wash their clothes and be ready by the third day, because on that day the Lord will come down on Mount Sinai in the sight of all the people." (Exodus 19:3-11)

Just as God blessed Abraham so that he could be used as an instrument to bless others, so also God asked the sons of Israel to be obedient so that He could use them to minister to the world!

This covenant was clearly a conditional covenant. God said; "... if you obey me fully and keep my covenant, then out of all nations you will be my treasured possession. Although the whole earth is mine, you will be for me a kingdom of priests and a holy nation...." Just as God blessed Abraham so that he could be used as an instrument to bless others, so also God asked the sons of Israel to be obedient so that He could use them to minister to the world.

We find the conditions of the Mosaic Covenant in the rest of the Old Testament Law: the remainder of Exodus, Leviticus, Numbers, and Deuteronomy. It included everything the people needed to be successful as a nation. It had a moral code, highlighted by the Ten Commandments. It included political systems for the time they were living under judges and for when they later had a king. It had an economic system that included a welfare plan. It even had a system of agrarian reform (every fiftieth year the land was to be redistributed to the original families). God also gave them dietary instructions that were vital for their survival when they wandered in the wilderness.

As previously mentioned, God wanted to use the nation of Israel as a kingdom of priests to minister to the rest of the world. Leviticus, chapter eighteen, reveals there was rampant incest, adultery, homosexuality, and bestiality among the people who were occupying the Promised Land. If the Israelites mingled and intermarried with them, they would become corrupted by their evil practices. God knew that for Israel to fulfill its destiny, the people needed to be holy and separated unto Him.

To fulfill God's calling and function as a kingdom of priests, Israel needed to be a holy nation!

So, God commanded the children of Israel to purge the land. This purging of the land was a judgment on the people in the land for their evil ways. But, more importantly, the purging of the land was so that Israel would be a holy people. God choose the children of Israel so that He could use them to minister to the world. To accomplish that purpose, they needed to be a holy people. Read God's command to the Israelites before they entered the land:

Completely destroy them -- the Hittites, Amorites, Canaanites, Perizzites, Hivites and Jebusites -- as the Lord your God has commanded you. Otherwise, they will teach you to follow all the detestable things they do in worshiping their gods, and you will sin against the Lord your God. (Deuteronomy 20:17-18)

Some "scholars" have been critical of the Old Testament because of this commandment. They try to contrast a God of love in the New Testament with a God of wrath in the Old Testament.

But, the Lord God is a holy God who must judge sin, and this judgment is not incompatible with His love for the sinner.

Warnings Before Entering Into the Land

In the book of Deuteronomy, Moses reviewed the law that was given at Sinai and during their wanderings. God called on them to be obedient and follow the law. Shortly before they entered the land, God reiterated His purpose for choosing them:

For you are a people holy to the Lord your God. The Lord your God has chosen you out of all the peoples on the face of the earth to be his people, his treasured possession.

The Lord did not set his affection on you and choose you because you were more numerous than other peoples, for you were the fewest of all peoples. But it was because the Lord loved you and kept the oath he swore to your forefathers that he brought you out with a mighty hand and redeemed you from the land of slavery, from the power of Pharaoh, king of Egypt. Know therefore that the Lord your God is God; he is the faithful God, keeping his covenant of love to a thousand generations of those who love him and keep his commands. (Deuteronomy 7:6-9)

These passages partially explain why God made Israel His chosen people. Both the Abrahamic and Mosaic Covenants emphasized that Israel was chosen so the people could be a blessing to the world -- that they would be a kingdom of priests to minister to the world.

At the end of their wanderings, God gave the children of Israel a final warning before entering into the land. God told them, through Moses, that if they were obedient when they entered into the land, they would be blessed. But, if they were disobedient, they would be cursed.

A king once asked his chaplain for evidence for the inspiration of the Bible. The chaplain pointed across the room to a man and replied, "There is your answer -- the Jew, your majesty." He was referring to the remarkable foretelling of the history of the Jews in a passage written hundreds of years before the events occurred. There are some amazing passages in Deuteronomy, chapters twenty-eight to thirty:

If you fully obey the Lord your God and carefully follow all his commands I give you today, the Lord your God will set you high above all the nations on earth. All these blessings will come upon you and accompany you if you obey the Lord your God: You will be blessed in the city and blessed in the country. The fruit of your womb will be blessed, and the crops of your land and the young of your livestock -- the calves of your herds and the lambs of your flocks. Your basket and your kneading trough will be blessed. You will be blessed when you come in and blessed when you go out... The Lord your God will bless you in the land he is giving you. The Lord will establish you as his holy people, as he promised you on oath, if you keep the commands of the Lord your God and walk in his ways.

Then all the peoples on earth will see that you are called by the name of the Lord, and they will fear you. The Lord will grant you abundant prosperity -- in the fruit of your womb, the young of your livestock and the crops of your ground -- in the land he swore to your forefathers to give you. The Lord will open the heavens, the storehouse of his bounty, to send rain on your land in season and to bless all the work of your hands. You will lend to many nations but will borrow from none. The Lord will make you the head, not the tail. If you pay attention to the commands of the Lord your God that I give you this day and carefully follow them, you will always be at the top, never at the bottom. Do not turn aside from any of the commands I give you today, to the right or to the left, following other gods and serving them. (Deuteronomy 28:1-14)

However, if you do not obey the Lord your God and do not carefully follow all his commands and decrees I am giving you today, all these curses will come upon you and overtake you: You will be cursed in the city and cursed in the country. Your basket and your kneading trough will be cursed. The fruit of your womb will be cursed, and the crops of your land, and the calves of your herds and the lambs of your flocks. You will be cursed when you come in and cursed when you go out.

The Lord will send on you curses, confusion and rebuke in everything you put your hand to, until you are destroyed and come to sudden ruin because of the evil you have done in forsaking him. (Deuteronomy 28:15-20)

In these passages, directed to the nation of Israel, God promised the people: If they were obedient, they would be blessed, but He also warned: if they were disobedient, they would be cursed. The Old Testament recorded their disobedience. One of the more common Old Testament pictures of the children of Israel was that of the unfaithful wife. The Israelites were consistently idolatrous.

It is important to understand that though Israelites wrote the Old Testament, they did not write a propaganda piece. It included the good, the bad, and the ugly. Outsiders did not describe the children of Israel as "the unfaithful wife." It was prophets of Israel who made this charge.

THE Old TESTAMENT, wriTTEN by ISRAEliTES, iNCludEd THE good, THE bad, ANd THE ugly AbOuT THEiR NATiON!

These warnings of consequences for disobedience were given by God, through Moses, before they even entered into the land. Later the children of Israel ignored these warnings, and thus they became prophetic. The curses followed their disobedience, and God used Moses to foretell the history of Israel -- thousands of years before the events transpired. The following passages tell of some of the curses that Moses warned would come upon them:

The Lord will cause you to be defeated before your enemies. You will come at them from one direction but flee from them in seven, and you will become a thing of horror to all the kingdoms on earth. (Deuteronomy 28:25)

Your sons and daughters will be given to another nation, and you will wear out your eyes watching for them day after day, powerless to lift a hand. (Deuteronomy 28:32)

The Lord will drive you and the king you set over you to a nation unknown to you or your fathers. There you will worship other gods, gods of wood and stone. You will become a thing of horror and an object of scorn and ridicule to all the nations where the Lord will drive you. (Deuteronomy 28:36-37)

You will have sons and daughters but you will not keep them, because they will go into captivity. (Deuteronomy 28:41)

All these curses will come upon you. They will pursue you and overtake you until you are destroyed, because you did not obey the Lord your God and observe the commands and decrees he gave you. They will be a sign and a wonder to you and your descendants forever. Because you did not serve the Lord your God joyfully and gladly in the time of prosperity, therefore in hunger and thirst, in nakedness and dire poverty, you will serve the enemies the Lord sends against you. He will put an iron yoke on your neck until he has destroyed you.

The Lord will bring a nation against you from far away, from the ends of the earth, like an eagle swooping down, a nation whose language you will not understand, a fierce-looking nation without respect for the old or pity for the young. They will devour the young of your livestock and the crops of your land until you are destroyed. They will leave you no grain, new wine or oil, nor any calves of your herds or lambs of your flocks until you are ruined. They will lay siege to all the cities throughout your land until the high fortified walls in which you trust fall down. They will besiege all the cities throughout the land the Lord your God is giving you.

Because of the suffering that your enemy will inflict on you during the siege, you will eat the fruit of the womb, the flesh of the sons and daughters the Lord your God has given you. Even the most gentle and sensitive man among you will have no compassion on his own brother or the wife he loves or his surviving children, and he will not give to one of them any of the flesh of his children that he is eating. It will be all he has left because of the suffering your enemy will inflict on you during the siege of all your cities. The most gentle and sensitive woman among you -- so sensitive and gentle that she would not venture to touch the ground with the sole of her foot -- will begrudge the husband she loves and her own son or daughter the afterbirth from her womb and the children she bears. For she intends to eat them secretly during the siege and in the distress that your enemy will inflict on you in your cities. If you do not carefully follow all the words of this law, which are written in this book, and do not revere this glorious and awesome name -- the Lord your God -- the Lord will send fearful plagues on you and your descendants, harsh and prolonged disasters ... (Deuteronomy 28:45-60)

You who were as numerous as the stars in the sky will be left but few in number, because you did not obey the Lord your God. Just as it pleased the Lord to make you prosper and increase in number, so it will please him to ruin and destroy you. You will be uprooted from the land you are entering to possess.

Then the Lord will scatter you among all nations, from one end of the earth to the other. There you will worship other gods -- gods of wood and stone, which neither you nor your fathers have known. Among those nations you will find no repose, no resting place for the sole of your foot. There the Lord will give you an anxious mind, eyes weary with longing, and a despairing heart. You will live in constant suspense, filled with dread both night and day, never sure of your life. In the morning you will say, "If only it were evening!" and in the evening, "If only it were morning!" -- because of the terror that will fill your hearts and the sights that your eyes will see. (Deuteronomy 28:62-67)

These are phenomenal passages in light of history. Think about it. Through Moses, God warned the Israelites they would be taken captive to a heathen land. Six hundred years later, they were taken captive to Babylon. By inference, the passage says that they would return to the land. Then, Moses warned, a second nation would attack them whose language they did not know. They understood the Aramaic language of the Babylonians, but they did not know the Latin spoken by the Romans. The prophecy foretold that when the second nation came there would be a siege so brutal that mothers would eat the flesh of their own (deceased) children. This is shocking to read. (God did not command it; He warned it would happen if they were disobedient.) The Jewish historian, Josephus, records that this happened when Titus brutally destroyed Jerusalem in seventy A.D., over one thousand years after the death of Moses -- just as Moses foretold.

Moses also warned the Israelites that they would be scattered all over the world, yet retain their national identity; and wherever they were scattered, they would suffer extreme persecution. This prophecy has been precisely fulfilled. Today there are American Jews, Russian Jews, German Jews, French Jews, and even some Oriental Jews. One can hardly go to any nation of the world and not find the Jew, and wherever the Israelites have been scattered, they have suffered persecution. The Holocaust is but one example of persecutions of the Jew in the nations where they have been scattered. The persecution of the scattered Jews is so well known that we even have a musical about it, The Fiddler on the Roof.

In Deuteronomy twenty-nine, (often called the Palestinian Covenant) Moses anticipated the question would later be asked: Why did this happen? Read how Moses answers it:

Your children who follow you in later generations and foreigners who come from distant lands will see the calamities that have fallen on the land and the diseases with which the Lord has afflicted it. The whole land will be a burning waste of salt and sulfur -- nothing planted, nothing sprouting, no vegetation growing on it. It will be like the destruction of Sodom and Gomorrah, Admah and Zeboiim, which the Lord overthrew in fierce anger. All the nations will ask: "Why has the Lord done this to this land? Why this fierce, burning anger?" And the answer will be: "It is because this people abandoned the covenant of the Lord, the God of their fathers, the covenant he made with them when He brought them out of Egypt. They went off and worshiped other gods and bowed down to them, gods they did not know, gods he had not given them. Therefore the Lord's anger burned against this land, so that he brought on it all the curses written in this book. In furious anger and in great wrath the Lord

uprooted them from their land and thrust them into another land, as it is now." (Deuteronomy 29:22-28).

It is important to understand that the Israelites are still scattered throughout the nations of the world because of their disobedience to the covenant God gave when they came out of *Egypt*, not *Haran*. They have been disobedient to the Mosaic Covenant, not the Abrahamic Covenant. There was nothing in the Abrahamic Covenant for them to disobey, other than the command to be circumcised, and that only applied to individuals, not the nation, and was rarely violated.

In Deuteronomy, chapters twenty-eight and twenty-nine, God gave thousand years of Israel's history in advance. This prophetic history is so accurate that many skeptics have questioned the Mosaic authorship and have tried to assign its authorship to a later date. (If one starts out with the assumption there is no personal God, and thus precise supernatural prophecy is impossible, these passages will obviously disrupt one's world view.) But, Joshua 8:30-35, records that the children of Israel read this exact part of Deuteronomy before they entered into the land, about 1200 B.C., hundreds of years before the earliest of these events transpired.

Moses recorded thousands of years of Israel's history before it happened!

Even if one accepts the latest possible dating for the writing of the Pentateuch (the first five books of the Bible), the prophetic fingerprints of God remain, because most of this prerecorded history transpired long after the latest date any scholar can possibly assign to these documents. (The latest dating given by skeptical scholars is just before the children of Israel were taken to Babylon in 586 B.C.) Remember, when the King asked for one evidence that God supernaturally inspired the Bible's human authors, the chaplain answered:

"The Jew, your majesty!"

The Unconditional Abrahamic Covenant Still Stands

But, the unconditional promises of the Abrahamic covenant still stand, in spite of the Israelites' disobedience, and we wait for God to finally fulfill the rest of His promise to Israel. Deuteronomy thirty-one tells us that God will ultimately **"circumcise their hearts,"** and return them to the land and bless them:

When all these blessings and curses I have set before you come upon you and you take them to heart wherever the Lord your God disperses you among the nations, and when you and your children return to the Lord your God and obey him with all your heart and with all your soul according to everything I command you today, then the Lord your God will restore your fortunes and have compassion on you and gather you again from all the nations where he scattered you.

Even if you have been banished to the most distant land under the heavens, from there the Lord your God will gather you and bring you back. He will bring you to the land that belonged to your fathers, and you will take possession of it. He will make you more prosperous and numerous than your fathers. The Lord your God will circumcise your hearts and the hearts of your descendants, so that you may love him with all your heart and with all your soul, and live. (Deuteronomy 30:1-8)

THE AbRAHAMIC ANd MOSAIC COVENANTS -- side by side

It is critical for a proper understanding of the Bible's plot, that one remembers that when the Children of Israel first entered into the land, on through the centuries, and even today, they have had these two primary covenants existing side by side. The *unconditional* Abrahamic Covenant promising that no matter what anyone else does, God will ultimately fulfill His promises to Abraham about the land, his seed (the Israelites), and the blessings for all families of the world. But, in the mean time, the *conditional* Mosaic Covenant is determining the status of the nation of Israel, and its enjoyment of God's promises.

Objections to Supernatural Prophecy Examined

It is important to understand the difference between a prediction and a prophecy. When people make predictions, they look at *this, this* and *this* and conclude *that* will happen in the future. A prophecy does not look at any current factors. It tells of a future, improbable event that will take place with no predisposing evidence.

Let me illustrate this principle: "If someone looked at all of the great basketball players at Duke University, and foretold that Duke would win a national championship, and it happened, that would be a prediction -- a good guess based on an astute observation. But, if someone foretold that Duke would win a national championship in football, *and it happened,* that would have to be a prophecy -- supernatural foreknowledge of a highly improbable event. Shortly after first using Duke in this illustration, a highly favored Duke basketball team was defeated by UConn in the national championship game. This illustrates the difficulty a false prophet faces when confronted with the Bible's requirement for 100% accuracy.

Biblical prophecy was **not** based on evidence that indicated probable future events. It was, and is, based on God's infinite foreknowledge!

It is often objected, "If enough prophecies are made, a few will be fulfilled." There is no doubt this is the strategy of some modern-day prophets. But, the Old Testament sets a high standard for anyone who would claim to be giving a prophecy from God, with a disastrous consequence for the impostor:

I will raise up a prophet from among their countrymen like you, and I will put My words in his mouth, and he shall speak to them all that I command him. And it shall come about that whoever will not listen to My words which he shall speak in My name, I Myself will require it of him. But the prophet who shall speak a word presumptuously in My name

which I have not commanded him to speak, or which he shall speak in the name of other gods, that prophet shall die. And you may say in your heart, "How shall we know the word which the Lord has not spoken?" When a prophet speaks in the name of the Lord, if the thing does not come about or come true, that is the thing which the Lord has not spoken. The prophet has spoken presumptuously; you shall not be afraid of him (Deuteronomy 18:18-22 NASB)

It is important to remember that the test for a prophet in Israel was 100% accuracy, and the penalty for failure was death by stoning. If today we still had the Old Testament test of 100% accuracy with the death penalty imposed on those who failed the test, there would be a lot fewer of the so-called modern-day prophets. And, those who still tried to make predictions would not last long!

The second objection is that it is all just "too improbable." But, it is important to remember that probability is affected by *purpose*. The biblical prophecies did not speak of random events. God had a specific purpose for speaking through the Old Testament prophets and telling, in advance, what He was going to do. It was a way He could verify for us that the message of the Bible is a true revelation from Himself.

THE OLD TESTAMENT REQUIRED 100% ACCURACY OF A PROPHET, AND probability is NOT RELEVANT WHEN THERE IS A PURPOSE!

The precise prophecies given by Moses about the future history of the children of Israel are only a few of the many Bible prophecies that have been fulfilled. The most amazing of all prophecies are those in the Old Testament pointing to the person of Jesus Christ as the Messiah. These prophecies reveal God's purpose in speaking through the prophets. As you read some of these prophecies (in the following chapters), remember: *at the time they were written, from a human perspective, they were far more improbable than Duke University winning the national collegiate football championship.*

Summary of Chapter Five:

After spending four hundred years in slavery in Egypt, God raised up a deliverer named Moses. Through Moses, God gave another covenant to the children of Israel. It is called the Mosaic Covenant. In this covenant, God told Israel He wanted to use them as a kingdom of priests, with the inference He wanted to use them to minister to the world. While the Abrahamic Covenant was unconditional, the Mosaic Covenant was clearly conditional. Its conditions were given in what is known as the Law. It included moral, political, economic, and religious provisions.

Before entering into the promised land, God warned the children of Israel, through Moses, that if they were disobedient to His commands in the Law, they would have curses come upon them. History records that they were disobedient. So Moses, in essence, became a prophet when he warned them of the curses. This warning, written hundreds of years before the events transpired, foretold the future history of Israel.

But, God's unconditional covenant with Abraham still stands, and based on it, Moses told there will be a future time when God will circumcise the hearts of the Israelites, gather them back from the lands where they would be scattered, and bless them.

The Bible required 100% accuracy of the prophets with the death penalty for false prophets, and biblical prophecies were not based on observations of factors that might lead to the prophecy being fulfilled. The unique supernatural nature of biblical prophecies are like fingerprints that God has left to confirm for us that He has spoken.

Chapter 6
The Law and The Promise

In the Abrahamic Covenant, God promised Abraham that his descendants would be so numerous they could not be counted, they would be given the land of Canaan, and through them all families of the earth would be blessed. As a result of a famine the children of Israel migrated to Egypt where they ended up in slavery. After about four hundred years in Egypt, God raised up a deliverer in the person of Moses, who led them out of Egypt.

At Mount Sinai, through Moses, the children of Israel entered into a covenant with God, known as the Mosaic Covenant, which gave them instructions for their personal and national lives. Before entering into the land, they were promised blessings if they followed these instructions, and they were warned of curses if they disobeyed them. As a result of their lack of trust in God to fulfill His promises, the children of Israel spent forty years wandering in the wilderness. Finally, they entered the land to possess it.

It is vital to see that the children of Israel had the Abrahamic and Mosaic covenants standing side by side as they entered into the Promised Land. The Abrahamic Covenant unconditionally promised the land, seed, and blessings. The conditional Mosaic Covenant told the Israelites that their present enjoyment of the land was dependent on their obedience.

A common error of interpretation is to take the conditions of the Mosaic Covenant and apply them to the Abrahamic

Covenant. But, in Galatians chapter three, the Apostle Paul warns that the conditions of the Mosaic Covenant are not conditions for the Abrahamic Covenant:

Therefore, be sure that it is those who are of faith that are sons of Abraham. And the Scriptures foreseeing that God would justify the Gentiles by faith, preached the gospel beforehand to Abraham, saying, "All the nations shall be blessed in you." So then those who are of faith are blessed with Abraham, the believer.

For as many as are of the works of the law are under a curse, for it is written, "Cursed is everyone who does not abide by all things written in the Book of the Law, to perform them." Christ redeemed us from the curse of the law, having become a curse for us -- for it is written "Cursed is every one who hangs on a tree" -- in order that in Christ Jesus the blessings of Abraham might come to the Gentiles, so that we might receive the promise of the Spirit through faith.

Brethren, I speak in terms of human relations: even though it is only a man's covenant, yet when it has been ratified, no one sets it aside of adds conditions to it. Now the promises were spoken to Abraham and to his seed. He does not say "And to seeds," as referring to many, but rather to one, "And to your seed," that is Christ. What I am saying is this: the Law, which came four hundred and thirty years later, does not invalidate a covenant previously ratified by God, so as to nullify the promise. (Galatians 3:7-17)

Paul's summary verse, Galatians 3:17, is one of the most important verses in the Bible from a theological standpoint, since it relates to the crucial question whether the Abrahamic Covenant is a conditional or unconditional covenant. It tells us; " **The law, which came 430 years later, does not invalidate a covenant previously ratified by God, so as to nullify the promise.**" The King James translation of this verse uses a "double negative" for emphasis. It says the Law **"cannot disannul, that it should make the promise of none effect."** This verse tells us that irrespective of what the law does, the Abrahamic Covenant still stands.

Before proceeding, we should note that while the Abrahamic Covenant places no conditions on its ultimate fulfillment, there is a condition, responding to God in faith, for individuals, and even for generations of Israelites, to be a part of the fulfillment of the Abrahamic covenant. It will ultimately be fulfilled based only on what God will do. The question is: Who will be the men and women of faith whom God will use to fulfill it? You could even say, "God is looking for *volunteers.*"

It is obvious from Galatians 3:14, and elsewhere, that the fulfillment of the "blessings" part of the Abrahamic Covenant was through Christ's death on the cross. There is a debate about the fulfillment of the promise for the land. (Many Bible scholars differ on this question. I will give my personal view on this issue in the last chapter of this book.) But, both sides of that debate agree it is through Jesus Christ that **all families of the earth are to be blessed.**

So, when Israel first entered into the land, they had two covenants, coexisting side by side. The unconditional Abrahamic Covenant promised land, seed, and blessings, and the conditional Mosaic Covenant warned Israel (the seed) that their present enjoyment of the land and the blessings was dependent on their being obedient to the Law that had been given through Moses.

WHEN ISRAEL ENTERED THE LAND, THEY HAD TWO MAIN COVENANTS. THE ABRAHAMIC COVENANT UNCONDITIONALLY PROMISED THEIR EVENTUAL POSSESSION OF THE LAND. THE MOSAIC COVENANT WARNED THAT THEIR PRESENT ENJOYMENT OF THE LAND WAS CONDITIONAL.

Because Galatians 3:17 asserts that the promises God made to Abraham still stand, a question naturally arises: "Why then did God give the Law?" The Apostle Paul was pretty sharp. He knew we would ask that question. So Paul himself asked it, and answered it:

Why the Law then? It was added because of transgressions, having been ordained through angels by the agency of

a mediator, until the seed should come to whom the promise had been made. Now a mediator is not for one party only; whereas God is only one. Is the Law then contrary to the promises of God? May it never be! For if a law had been given which was able to impart life, then righteousness would indeed have been based on law.

But the Scripture has shut up all men under sin, that the promise by faith in Jesus Christ might be given to those who believe. But before faith came, we were kept in custody under the law, being shut up to the faith which was later to be revealed. Therefore the Law has become our tutor to lead us to Christ, that we may be justified by faith. But now that faith has come, we are no longer under a tutor. (Galatians 3:19-25)

In Paul's answer, he said the purpose of the Law was to instruct -- to **"shut up"** men to faith. The Apostle Paul also expressed this idea in Romans 3:19, where it said the law was given **"that every mouth may be silenced."** A good paraphrase of these verses would be --

"The Law was Given to Shut Their Mouths!"

You ask, 'How does the Law shut one's mouth?' It's a common practice for men and women to say; "I'm a pretty good person. I have not done anything wrong!" When someone says, "I'm not guilty," Paul suggests a look at the Law, and the Law shouts:

"Oh shut up! You are guilty. You have violated God's law!"

In Romans seven, Paul goes even further. He says the Law will cause us to sin. Let's see how this can happen. Assume that you have two identical houses, on different streets, but in the same subdivision. Both have a big plate glass window facing the street. There is just one difference. One window has a sign in it that says, "Do not throw rocks at this window." Guess which window is most likely to get broken. That's right! When we read the sign, our likely response is to start looking for a rock and say to ourselves, "Who says I can't throw a rock at that window?" The "thou shall not" produces instant rebellion in our sinful nature and when we respond defiantly, it exposes our sinful nature. Paul explains the Law's function in Romans 7:13:

Therefore did that which is good (the law) **become a cause of death for me? May it never be! Rather it was sin, in order that it might be shown to be sin by effecting my death through that which is good, that through the commandment sin might become utterly sinful.**

The law thus serves a diagnostic function. When I was an officer in the infantry, they taught us the first thing we needed to do when we *dug in* was to make an *estimate of the situation.* We were told that our very lives could depend on whether we made an *accurate* estimate of the situation. If we tried to be positive, and just ignored the aggressors across from us, we would get clobbered.

God knows that we need to make an accurate estimate of the situation in our personal lives. He knows that for us to see our need, we must first understand that God's law is righteous and just, and that we are sinful and guilty before Him. Our natural tendency is to try and defend and justify our sinful behavior. But, when we try to say how good we are, the Law shouts at us, *"Oh, shut up!"*

Today, there are many who believe there are no absolutes. There are even some who will imply they are *absolutely sure* there are no absolutes. In the Bible, God tells us they are wrong! In the ten commandments, and other biblical admonitions, God gives us knowledge of rights and wrongs that emanate from His holy nature. When we honestly examine God's law, we all know we are guilty. The Bible tells us, **"The fool hath said in his heart, There is no God."** (Psalms 14:1 KJV). We could add, it is equally foolish to deny God's standards of right and wrong, and even more foolish to deny our sin and guilt.

Paul continues on in his letter to the Galatians and says; **"Therefore, the Law has become our tutor to lead us to Christ, that we may be justified by faith."** (Galatians 3:24) But, you ask, how could the Law lead us to Christ? After all, Moses wrote it more than a thousand years before Jesus was even born! In the story line (chapter two in this book) we saw that

God gave two things at Mount Sinai: the law and the pattern for the Tabernacle!

The Earthly Tabernacle Depicts the Heavenly Tabernacle

Through Moses, God gave instructions to the children of Israel on how to deal with their sin problem. When they sinned, they were to bring a sacrifice to the Tabernacle, or after it was constructed, to the Temple. The New Testament book of Hebrews, chapters eight and nine, reveals that the earthly Tabernacle was a copy and shadow of the heavenly Tabernacle, the dwelling place of God. The instructions for meeting God at the Tabernacle were given through Moses in the Book of Leviticus. Leviticus chapter three is but one of several passages in Leviticus where we find God's instructions:

If he offers an animal from the flock as a fellowship offering to the Lord, he is to offer a male or female without defect. If he offers a lamb, he is to present it before the Lord. He is to lay his hand on the head of his offering and slaughter it in front of the Tent of Meeting. Then Aaron's sons shall sprinkle its blood against the altar on all sides. From the fellowship offering he is to bring a sacrifice made to the Lord by fire: its fat, the entire fat tail cut off close to the backbone, all the fat that covers the inner parts or is connected to them, both kidneys with the fat on them near the loins, and the covering of the liver, which he will remove with the kidneys. The priest shall burn them on the altar as food, an offering made to the Lord by fire. (Leviticus 3:6-11)

In the book of Leviticus, the sacrifice could have been a bull, a lamb, or a goat. (For illustrative purposes we will use a lamb.) When a Jew wanted to be at peace with God, he was to bring a lamb to the entrance of the Tabernacle, lay his hands on the head of the lamb, kill the lamb, and then have a priest sprinkle its blood on the altar.

When a Jew brought the lamb to the tabernacle, and laid his hands on the head of the lamb, it was a picture of two things. First, it was a picture of identification. He was saying, "God, I want you to see me and this lamb as <u>one</u>. I am identified with this lamb!" The second picture was that of transference. He was saying, "God, all that is true of me is true of this lamb, and all that is true of this lamb is true of me."

Putting it in the first person, if all that is true of me, is true of the lamb, what happens to my sin when I lay my hands on the head of the lamb? That's right, my sin is transferred to the lamb. What happens to the lamb's sin? It is transferred, ... wait a minute, lambs don't sin. And, this lamb had to be <u>perfect</u>, without any blemish.

When an Israelite placed his hands on the head of the lamb, he was identifying with the lamb and portraying his sin as being transferred to the lamb. Then he was to kill the lamb. Romans 6:23 says, **"The wages of sin is death..."** And, Hebrews 9:22 teaches us **"... all things are cleansed with blood, and without shedding of blood there is no forgiveness."**

This is part of what is often called the *scarlet cord of redemption*. This scarlet cord weaves all the way through the Bible. It can be found in so many passages, it is not practical to attempt to record all of them in this book, but we will look at a few of them. The scarlet cord started in Genesis, chapters three and four. When one reads between the lines, it is obvious that God had given instructions for sacrifices to Cain and Able. In Genesis twenty-two, a passage we looked at in chapter four of this book, God provided a sacrifice when Abraham was tested. God provided a ram as a substitute for his son Isaac that was offered as a sacrifice. When God delivered the children of Israel from Egypt, blood was placed on their doorposts, and the Jews still observe the Feast of Passover in remembrance of what God did for them.

THERE IS A SCARLET CORD OF REDEMPTION THAT RUNS ALL OF THE WAY THROUGH THE BIBLE.

Isaiah fifty-three is one of the Bible's great chapters. I once talked to a girl who grew up in a Jewish family who shared with me that her father had attended a service in a synagogue where they skipped over the fifty-third chapter, as they were reading the Book of Isaiah. Wondering why, as he sat in the synagogue, he read Isaiah, chapter fifty-three, in his Hebrew Bible. He realized Jesus was and is the Messiah, and after further study, her father became a Christian. The following is the text of this great chapter from *The Holy Scriptures* published by the Jewish Publication Society of America. Many scholars feel chapter fifty-three should start at Isaiah 52:13, where we will begin:

Behold, my servant will prosper, He will be exalted and lifted up and shall be very high. According as many were appalled at thee-- So marred was his visage unlike that of a man, And his form unlike that of the sons of men-- So shall he startle many nations, Kings will shut their mouths because of Him. For that which had not been told them they will see, and what they have not heard, they will perceive.

Who would have believed our report? And to whom hath the arm of the Lord been revealed? For he shot up right forth as a sapling, And as a root out of dry ground; He had no form or comeliness that we should look upon Him. Nor beauty that we should delight in Him. He was despised and forsaken of men, a man of pains, and acquainted with disease, and as one from whom men hide their face, he was despised, and we esteemed him not.

Surely our disease he did bare, and our pains he carried; Whereas we esteemed Him stricken, Smitten of God and afflicted. But He was wounded because of our transgressions, He was crushed because of our iniquities; the chastisement of our welfare was upon him, and with his stripes we were healed.

All we like sheep did go astray, We turned every one to his own way; And the Lord hath made to light on him the iniquity of us all. He was oppressed, though he humbled himself, And opened not His mouth; As a lamb that is lead to the slaughter, and as a sheep that before its shearers is dumb; Yea, he opened not his mouth. By oppression and judgment He was taken away. And with his generation who did reason? For he was cut off out of the land of the living, For the transgression of my people to whom the stroke was due. And they made his grave with the wicked, And with

the rich in His tomb; Although He had done no violence, Neither was any deceit in His mouth.

Yet it pleased the Lord to crush him by disease (Note: The Hebrew word *chalah*, translated *disease*, can also be translated *a wound*); **to see if his soul would offer itself in restitution, That he might see his seed, prolong his days, And that the purpose of the Lord might prosper by his hand. Of the travail of his soul he shall see to the full, even My servant, Who by his knowledge did justify the Righteous One to the many, and their iniquities he did bear.**

Therefore I will divide him a portion among the great, and He shall divide the spoil with the mighty, Because he bared his soul unto death, And was numbered with the transgressors. Yet He bore the sin of many, and made intercession for the transgressors. (Isaiah 52:13 - 53:12 JPS)

Then Isaiah adds an interesting comment, **"For thy Maker is thy husband, The Lord of hosts is His name; and the Holy One of Israel is thy redeemer, The God of the whole earth shall He be called."** (Isaiah 54:5 JPS - (This Jewish translation identifies the suffering servant of the preceding chapter as the Holy One of Israel -- the God of the whole earth.)

There is no doubt that Isaiah fifty-three prophetically describes the life and death of Jesus. (This will be more obvious when we examine some passages in Isaiah about "the Holy One of Israel" in the next chapter of this book.) As in Leviticus, Isaiah describes the principles of identification and transference. Read a few of the key verses from Isaiah fifty-three in the beautiful language of the King James Translation:

All we like sheep have gone astray, we have turned everyone to his own way, and the Lord has laid on Him the iniquity of us all... Yet it pleased the Lord to bruise Him, He hath put Him to grief; when thou shalt make His soul an offering for sin. (Isaiah 53:6 & 10 KJV)

The Promised "Lamb of God" is Jesus!

Later, in the New Testament, John the Baptist referred to Isaiah when he said; **"as it is written in the book of the words of Isaiah."** (Luke 3:4) Then, when Jesus came to him, John pointed and said; **"Behold the Lamb of God who takes away the sin of the world!"** (John 1:29).

During His earthly ministry, Jesus said; **"... the Son of Man** (His favorite name for Himself) **came not to be ministered unto, but to minister and give His life a ransom for the many"** (Mark 10:45 KJV). There are two key words in the original Greek language in this verse: the words translated *ransom* and *for*. *Ransom*, of course, refers to a payment to obtain release of a captive. The word *for* could be translated "in the place of." So we see that Jesus, the Messiah, came as **"the Lamb of God,"** and offered Himself as our substitute, dying on the cross, in our place, for our sin, to secure our freedom.

Jesus expressed this to us in the last words He said on the cross when He said; **"It is finished!"** (John 19:30) In the original Greek language, the words used were the exact words used in those days to write across the face of a bill, **"Paid in Full."** This is the heart and soul of what is called the Gospel. The Good News is that Jesus, the Lamb of God, came, died on the cross as our substitute, and paid <u>in full</u> the price for our sins.

The Apostle Paul expressed the same thing when he wrote **"He made Him who knew no sin to be sin on our behalf, that we might become the righteousness of God in Him."** (II Corinthians 5:21) Paul's picture is of our sin being transferred to Jesus, and His righteousness being imputed (given) to us.

Remember, in the illustration God gave through the sacrifices required in the book of Leviticus, all that is true of the lamb is also true of the person laying their hands on the lamb. So, we stand as ones who are righteous before God. But, our righteousness is not of ourselves. It is a gift from God. In the Bible this is often called *grace*, a term that means *unmerited favor*. And yes -- it is amazing!

Back to the book of Leviticus for another of God's illustrations that point to Jesus. In chapter sixteen, God gave the children of Israel instructions they were to observe one day every year. The observance is called The Day of Atonement. On that day, Moses told the Israelites to take two goats and cast lots on them to determine one goat for the Lord and one for a *scape-*

goat. Then they were commanded to lay their hands on the head of the first goat, kill it, and offer it as a sacrifice for their sin. Read the instructions God gave them for the second goat:

He is to lay both hands on the head of the live goat and confess over it all the wickedness and rebellion of the Israelites -- all their sins -- and put them on the goat's head. He shall send the goat away into the desert in the care of a man appointed for the task. The goat will carry on itself all their sins to a solitary place; and the man shall release it in the desert. (Leviticus 16:21-22)

The "Good News" -- God forgives and forgets our sin!

This passage about the scapegoat is a picture of the Good News, that after we have our sins transferred to Jesus, the Lamb of God, God not only forgives -- He also forgets our sin. **"For I will be merciful to their iniquities, and I will remember their sins no more."** (Hebrews 8:12)

The national hero of Chechyna, a former province of the Soviet Union, was a man named Chemiel. During the time of the Czars, he led a band of Chechen men, women, and children who resisted the Czar, and carried out guerrilla attacks on the Czar's army. Chemiel's group had strict rules of conduct, including a rule that said, "Thou shall not steal!" The penalty for violating this rule was forty lashes with a whip.

One day, stealing broke out in the camp. A few days later, they found out who did the stealing. *The thief was Chemiel's mother!* Consequently, Chemiel had a major problem. If he was to have justice, he had to give the command and see his mother, whom he dearly loved, lashed forty times with a whip. But, if he did not have justice, he would not be able to discipline anyone else in the future. He knew, if he did not have his mother whipped, they would lose their ability to operate effectively as a unit, and chances are the Czar's army would capture them all.

Chemiel probably tossed and turned at night as he thought about his paradox. But, the next morning he made his decision. He realized justice had to be served. He had them bring out his mother -- he gave the command, and they began to lash her. But, after the third lash, Chemiel found his answer. He had them stop. He took his mother's place and Chemiel took the remaining thirty-seven lashes on his own back. This is an example of a man's love for his mother. But, in John 3:16, the Bible tells us what God, in Christ, did for us:

For God so loved the world that He gave His only begotten Son, that whosoever believeth in Him should not perish but have everlasting life.

The heart and soul of the Gospel is that Jesus, the Messiah, came to die on the cross, as the Lamb of God, for our sins.

When properly comprehended, there is no boasting in the Christian life. Paul writes in Ephesians 2:8-9, **"For by grace (unmerited favor) you have been saved through faith; and that not of yourselves, it is the gift of God, not as a result of works, that no one should boast."**

I see myself as being in a nearly identical position with Chemiel's mother. Because of what she did, her son had to take the lashes on his back. So also, as a result of what I have done, Jesus died on the cross in my place. But, Chemiel's mother could hold her head high. The penalty for her sin was paid by her son. So also, as Christians, we can hold our heads high because Jesus, the Son of God, paid in full the price for our sin. God in His holiness could not merely overlook our sin. Since He loves us, He sent Jesus to die in our place for our sin.

But, the Good News does not end there -- the tomb could not hold the Lamb of God who died for our sin. He rose victorious on that first Easter Sunday morning. In our identification with Him, He not only died for us, but He now shares with us His resurrected life, **"... which is Christ in you, the hope of glory"** (Colossians 1:27).

The apostle John assures us that we can know for certain that we have received the gift of eternal life:

And the witness is this, that God has given us eternal life, and this life is in His Son. He who has the Son has the life; he who does not have the Son of God does not have the life. These things I have written to you who believe in the name of the Son of God, in order that you may know that you have eternal life. (I John 5:11-13)

In his book, The Temple, Alfred Edersheim tells us what the Jews prayed, in Old Testament times, when they laid their hands on the head of a sacrificial lamb. They prayed:

> Oh God, I have sinned, I have rebelled, I have done perversely, I have (they would name the sin), but I return in repentance to You. Let this one (the lamb) be for my atonement.

If you have never placed your faith in Jesus as your personal Lamb of God, who died on the cross for your sin, visually picture yourself with your hands placed on Jesus. Identify yourself as being one with Him, and pray from your heart, with words similar to those prayed by the Israelites of old, saying:

> Oh God, I have sinned, I have rebelled, I have done perversely, I am a sinner, I have ... (you may have a particular sin you need to name and confess). But, I turn in repentance to you. Let Jesus, the Lamb of God, be for my atonement. And, Jesus, come and live in my life as my personal Savior and Lord! Thank you Jesus, for hearing my prayer. Thank you God for forgiving me and for sending your Son, Jesus, to live in me. In Jesus' name, Amen!

When you honestly and sincerely place your faith in Jesus, God promises He will forgive and forget your sins, Jesus will come and dwell within you, and you will become a child of God -- a possessor of eternal life. This is one of the central teachings of the Bible's plot, and it's really -- **"Good News!"**

SUMMARY OF CHAPTER SIX:

The children of Israel had two covenants existing side by side. The unconditional Abrahamic Covenant promising land, seed, and blessings, and the conditional Mosaic Covenant warning them that their present enjoyment of the land was based on their obedience. They are two separate covenants, and the conditions of the Mosaic Covenant cannot be applied to the Abrahamic Covenant because, as Paul pointed out, the law was given four hundred and thirty years later and does not annul the promise.

The question naturally arises, "Why then was the law given?" Paul asked that question and answered it himself in Galatians, chapter three, when he explained that the law was given to reveal to men their sin and be a schoolmaster that would lead them to Christ that they might be justified by faith.

In answer to the question how the law, written over a thousand years before Christ was born, could lead people to Christ, one should look at the Levitical sacrifices that were given as part of God's Law. This sacrificial system pictured, and a prophecy in Isaiah foretold, that the Holy One of Israel, the Messiah, would come as a suffering Savior and pour out His soul an offering for sin. These passages pointed to the ultimate sacrifice that would be offered for our sin when Jesus, the Lamb of God, died on the cross so our sins can be forgiven and we can inherit eternal life.

Date: _____

I, _____, do affirm that I have placed my faith in Jesus Christ, the Lamb of God, who died on the cross in my place and for my sin. Jesus is my Savior and Lord.

Thank you Jesus,

Signed: _____

Chapter 7
Someone is Coming!

In the Book of Joshua, the children of Israel conquered the land. But, they disobeyed God's commands to purge the land of its inhabitants, to not intermarry with them, and to not worship their gods (Judges 3:5-6). Consequently, they went through the ups and downs recorded in the book of Judges. The last judge was Samuel. The children of Israel were concerned when Samuel appointed his evil sons as judges, and they did not want Samuel's sons to rule Israel after his death, so they asked for a king (I Samuel 8). After being warned that a king would dominate and tax them, the children of Israel responded: **"We want a king over us. Then we will be like the other nations, with a king to lead us and go out before us and fight our battles."** (I Samuel 8:19-20)

God consented, and gave them Saul as their first king. Because of his disobedience, the kingship was later removed from Saul and his descendants. The second king was David. He was the great conquering king. After winning some battles, David returned to his palace, and a very important event took place that is recorded in II Samuel chapter seven:

The Davidic Covenant

After the king was settled in his palace and the Lord had given him rest from all his enemies around him, he said to Nathan the prophet, "Here I am, living in a palace of cedar, while the ark of God remains in a tent." Nathan replied to the king, "Whatever you have in mind, go ahead and do it, for the Lord is with you."

That night the word of the Lord came to Nathan, saying: "Go and tell my servant David, 'This is what the Lord says: Are you the one to build me a house to dwell in? I have not dwelt in a house from the day I brought the Israelites up out of Egypt to this day. I have been moving from place to place with a tent as My dwelling. Wherever I have moved with all the Israelites, did I ever say to any of their rulers whom I commanded to shepherd my people Israel, "Why have you not built me a house of cedar?" Now then, tell my servant David, 'This is what the Lord Almighty says: I took you from the pasture and from following the flock to be ruler over my people Israel. I have been with you wherever you have gone, and I have cut off all your enemies from before you.

Now I will make your name great, like the names of the greatest men of the earth. And I will provide a place for my people Israel and will plant them so that they can have a home of their own and no longer be disturbed. Wicked people will not oppress them anymore, as they did at the beginning and have done ever since the time I appointed leaders over my people Israel. I will also give you rest from all your enemies.

The Lord declares to you that the Lord Himself will establish a house for you: When your days are over and you rest with your fathers, I will raise up your offspring to succeed you, who will come from your own body, and I will establish his kingdom. He is the one who will build a house for my name, and I will establish the throne of his kingdom forever. I will be his father, and he will be my son. When he does wrong, I will punish him with the rod of men, with floggings inflicted by men. But my love will never be taken away from him, as I took it away from Saul, whom I removed from before you. Your house and your kingdom will endure forever before me; your throne will be established forever." (II Samuel 7:1-16)

This passage records a covenant that God made with David. It's called the Davidic Covenant. While there were personal promises for David, and promises for his people, we focus on the promises in verses twelve through sixteen. God promised David that the kingship would never be removed from his descendants, as it had been from King Saul, and that his *house*, his *kingdom*, and his *throne* would endure forever.

Psalm eighty-nine also explained the Davidic Covenant:

I will sing of the Lord's great love forever; with my mouth I will make Your faithfulness known through all generations. I will declare that your love stands firm forever, that you established your faithfulness in heaven itself. You said, "I have made a covenant with my chosen one, I have sworn to David my servant, 'I will establish your line forever and make your throne firm through all generations.'" ...

Indeed, our shield belongs to the Lord, our king to the Holy One of Israel. Once You spoke in a vision, to your faithful people you said: "I have bestowed strength on a warrior; I have exalted a young man from among the people. I have found David my servant; with my sacred oil I have anointed him. My hand will sustain him; surely my arm will strengthen him. No enemy will subject him to tribute; no wicked man will oppress him. I will crush his foes before him and strike down his adversaries.

My faithful love will be with him, and through my name his horn will be exalted. I will set his hand over the sea, his right hand over the rivers. He will call out to me, 'You are my Father, my God, the Rock my Savior.' I will also appoint him my firstborn, the most exalted of the kings of the earth. I will maintain my love to him forever, and my covenant with him will never fail. I will establish his line forever, his throne as long as the heavens endure. If his sons forsake my law and do not follow my statutes, if they violate my decrees and fail to keep my commands, I will punish their sin with the rod, their iniquity with flogging; but I will not take my love from him, nor will I ever betray my faithfulness. I will not violate my covenant or alter what my lips have uttered. Once for all, I have sworn by my holiness -- and I will not lie to David -- that his line will continue forever and his throne endure before me like the sun; it will be established forever like the moon, the faithful witness in the sky."

In verse eighteen the Davidic kingship is referred to as **"the Holy One of Israel,"** and in verse twenty it says, **"I have found David My servant; with My sacred oil I have anointed him."**

The word *Messiah* means *the Anointed One.* The Davidic Covenant lays the foundation for God's promises to Israel that He would send them a Messiah. This theme resounds throughout the Old Testament prophets. Like the Abrahamic Covenant, the Davidic Covenant is unconditional!

The Davidic Covenant is the foundation for the Promise to Israel of a coming Messiah.

The promise of "One who would come," who would provide redemption, was first mentioned way back in the Garden of Eden. There, God said He would provide victory through a descendant of Eve (Genesis 3:15). At that point, the *One who would come and provide redemption* could have been anyone from the whole human race. The rest of the Bible progressively narrows it down.

It was narrowed down to a descendant of Noah by, what could be called, "a process of elimination." Then in Genesis twelve it was narrowed down to a descendant of Abraham through whom God would provide blessings for all families of the earth. It was successively narrowed down to descendants of Isaac and Jacob. Then in Genesis 49:10 we learn that the scepter (a symbol of rulership) was restricted to the tribe of Judah. Then, as we pointed out above, in II Samuel seven **"the coming One"** is to be a descendant of King David.

All through the Old Testament the Prophets proclaim, "He is coming!" -- "The Messiah is coming!" -- "The King is coming!" He will be of the **house** of King David and He will rule over the **kingdom** from the **throne** of David.

Solomon followed David as king. After Solomon's death, his son Rehoboam became king, he raised the taxes, Jeroboam led a rebellion; and the kingdom was divided into Northern and Southern kingdoms. First the Northern Kingdom was taken captive to Assyria, and later the Southern Kingdom was taken to Babylon. Finally, as explained in "The Story Line" (Chapter Two of this book), the Southern Kingdom was allowed to return to Jerusalem and rebuild the Temple and the wall.

The Message of the Old Testament Prophets

During all of this time, except for a few short interludes, the children of Israel were in rebellion against God and the kingdom was in decline. During this era, the Lord raised up prophets to speak to the nation. A survey of the prophetic books in the Old Testament reveals five elements were common in most of their messages to the people:

1. They rebuked the nation by pointing out its sin and rebellion.
2. They called on the children of Israel to repent and return to the original "constitution" that had been given through Moses.
3. They warned of divine judgment to follow if they did not repent and return to the Lord.
4. They reasserted eternal promises from God (mostly related to the Abrahamic and Davidic Covenants).
5. They told of future blessings that would be part of a kingdom that would be established when Messiah, the King, comes. The promised King and His kingdom were promised for the benefit of both Israel and the world.

In the last two elements, the main themes of the prophets were that the King is coming and that Israel will be blessed. The prophetic message of the coming King and the blessings on the nation of Israel are inextricably intertwined. The prophets also emphasized that through Israel's Messiah, all families of the world will be blessed.

THE PROPHETIC MESSAGE OF THE COMING KING AND THE BLESSINGS ON THE NATION OF ISRAEL ARE INEXTRICABLY INTERTWINED.

We saw in Psalm eighty-nine that the promised Messiah was referred to as **the Lord, our king to the Holy One of Israel** (Psalms 89:18). The book of Isaiah refers over thirty times to **the Holy One of Israel.** Chapter five, verse twenty-four, sets the tone where it says, **"For they have rejected the law of the Lord Almighty and spurned the word of the Holy One of Israel."** The broad context of Isaiah tells us this is a reference to the promised Messiah.

The "Holy One of Israel" Will be God Who Became Man

Isaiah 7:14 tells of the coming One: **"Therefore the Lord himself will give you a sign; The virgin will be with child and will give birth to a son, and will call him Immanuel."** The word *Immanuel* means "God is with us." Here we see the promised one is to be a man, who is born of a virgin, *but who is God.* Isaiah 9:6-7 repeats this thought in a great passage that is magnificently put to music in Handel's Messiah:

For unto us a child is born, unto us a son is given, and the government shall be upon His shoulder: and His name shall be called Wonderful Counselor, the Mighty God, the Everlasting Father, the Prince of Peace. Of the increase of His government and peace there shall be no end, upon the throne of David, and upon his kingdom, to order it, and to establish with judgment and with justice from henceforth even for ever. The zeal of the Lord of hosts will perform this. (Isaiah 9:6-7 KJV)

Notice this passage proclaimed that He will be physically born, yet be **"Mighty God,"** and He will sit **"on David's throne."** The teaching that Jesus was "... **the Word** (God) **became flesh and dwelt among us"** (John 1:14) did not originate in the New Testament. It is clear that many passages in the prophetic books proclaimed the coming Messiah will be a descendant of King David, but will also be the Lord God. The New Testament book of Philippians, chapter two, explains this more fully:

Have this attitude in yourselves which was also in Christ Jesus, who, although He existed in the form of God, did not regard equality with God a thing to be grasped, but emptied Himself, taking the form of a bondservant, and being made in the likeness of men, and being found in appearance as a man, He humbled Himself by becoming obedient to the point of death, even death on a cross. Therefore also God highly exalted Him and bestowed on Him the name which is above every name, that at the name of Jesus every knee should bow, of those who are in heaven and under the earth, and that every tongue confess that Jesus Christ is Lord, to the glory of God the Father. (Philippians 2:5-11)

In Isaiah 11:1-5, the fact that **"the Coming One"** will be a descendant of King David is again proclaimed, when He is referred to as a **"Stem of Jesse"** (David's father) with **"roots"** in the Davidic line, **"and that the Spirit of the Lord will rest on him"** ... With righteousness he will judge the poor, ... And with the breath of his lips he will slay the wicked." Isaiah 11:10 says there will be a time when the Gentiles will seek the **"root out of Jesse and his resting place will be glorious"** (a veiled reference to His resurrection and the empty tomb). Read more selected verses from the prophet Isaiah:

In love a throne will be established; in faithfulness a man will sit on it -- one from the house of David -- one who in judging seeks justice and speeds the cause of righteousness. (16:5)

For the Lord Almighty will reign on Mount Zion and in Jerusalem ... (Isaiah 24:23.)

Once more the humble will rejoice in the Lord; the needy will rejoice in the Holy One of Israel (Isaiah 29:19).

Be strong, do not fear; your God will come, he will come with vengeance; with divine retribution he will come to save you. Then will the eyes of the blind be opened and the ears of the deaf unstopped. Then will the lame leap like a deer, and the mute tongue shout for joy. Water will gush forth in the wilderness and streams in the desert. (Isaiah 35:4-6).

"... for I myself will help you," declares the Lord your **Redeemer, the Holy One of Israel** (Isaiah 41:14).

Here is my servant, whom I uphold, my chosen one in whom I delight; I will put my Spirit on him and he will bring justice to the nations. He will not shout or cry out, or raise his voice in the streets. A bruised reed he will not break, and a smoldering wick he will not snuff out. In faithfulness he will bring forth justice; He will not falter or be discouraged till he establishes justice on earth. In his law the islands will put their hope. (Isaiah 42:1-4)

For I am the Lord your God, the Holy One of Israel, your Savior (Isaiah 43:3).

This is what the Lord says -- Israel's King and Redeemer, the Lord Almighty: I am the first and I am the last; apart

from me there is no God. Who then is like me? Let him proclaim it. Let him declare and lay out before me what has
happened since I established my ancient people, and what is
yet to come -- yes, let him foretell what will come. (Isaiah
44:6-7)

I will also make you a light for the Gentiles, that you
may bring my salvation to the ends of the earth. This is
what the Lord says -- the Redeemer and Holy One of Israel
-- to him who was despised and abhorred by the nation, to
the servant of rulers: "Kings will see you and rise up,
princes will see and bow down, because of the Lord, who is
faithful, the Holy One of Israel, who has chosen you."
(Isaiah 49:6-7)

I will make your oppressors eat their own flesh; they will
be drunk on their own blood, as with wine. Then all mankind
will know that I, the Lord, am your Savior, your Redeemer, the
Mighty One of Jacob." (Isaiah 49:26)

These quotations from the prophet Isaiah tell us that the
One who is coming will be a descendent of King David, yet He is
the Lord God of Israel, and through Him the nations of the world
will be blessed. They tell us that the Messiah will be our
Redeemer and Savior. In the last chapter we looked at Isaiah,
chapter fifty-three, a comprehensive prophecy about the coming
Messiah. Using a Jewish translation, it described Him as **"despised
and we esteemed him not..."** and **"he bore the sin of many."**

In that great chapter, Isaiah explains God's ultimate purpose
for sending His Messiah. God had promised to bless all families
of the earth through a descendant of Abraham, Isaac, Jacob, and
David. The blessings promised in the Abrahamic and Davidic
Covenants point to what God would do through a descendant of
Abraham and David to provide redemption for sin. But, in addi-
tion to the prophecy that He would be a suffering Savior, Isaiah
also proclaims the coming Messiah will be a victorious king who
will establish a righteous rule from Zion (Israel):

The glory of Lebanon will come to you, the pine, the fir and
the cypress together, to adorn the place of my sanctuary; and I
will glorify the place of my feet. The sons of your oppressors
will come bowing before you; all who despise you will bow

down at your feet and will call you the City of the Lord, Zion of the Holy One of Israel. ... You will drink the milk of nations and be nursed at royal breasts. Then you will know that I, the Lord, am your Savior, your Redeemer, the Mighty One of Jacob. ... No longer will violence be heard in your land, nor ruin or destruction within your borders, but you will call your walls Salvation and your gates Praise. ... the Lord will be your everlasting light, and your days of sorrow will end. Then will all your people be righteous and they will possess the land forever." (Isaiah 60:13-21)

THE ONE who is coming is A descendant of King David, yet He is the Lord God of Israel, and through Him the nations of the world will be blessed.

See, the Lord is coming with fire, and his chariots are like a whirlwind; He will bring down his anger with fury, and his rebuke with flames of fire. For with fire and with his sword the Lord will execute judgment upon all men, and many will be those slain by the Lord....

"And I, because of their actions and their imaginations, am about to come and gather all nations and tongues, and they will come and see my glory. I will set a sign among them, and I will send some of those who survive to the nations -- to Tarshish, to the Libyans and Lydians (famous as archers), to Tubal and Greece, and to the distant islands that have not heard of my fame or seen my glory. They will proclaim my glory among the nations.

And they will bring all your brothers, from all the nations, to my holy mountain in Jerusalem as an offering to the Lord -- on horses, in chariots and wagons, and on mules and camels," says the Lord. "They will bring them, as the Israelites bring their grain offerings, to the temple of the Lord in ceremonially clean vessels. And I will select some of them also to be priests and Levites," says the Lord. "As the new heavens and the new earth that I make will endure before me," declares the Lord, "so will your name and descendants

endure. From one New Moon to another and from one Sabbath to another, all mankind will come and bow down before me," says the Lord. (Isaiah 66:18-23)

Not only Isaiah, but the other prophets proclaimed, "He is coming!" "The Messiah is coming!" "The King is coming!" Though they were written during a time when the disobedience of the children of Israel was rampant, after warning of judgment for sin, the prophetic writings inevitably told of future blessings through the promised Messiah.

Micah 5:2 announced He would be born in Bethlehem; **"But as for you, Bethlehem Ephrathah, too little to be among the clans of Judah, from you One will go forth for Me to be ruler in Israel. His goings forth are from long ago, from the days of eternity.... And He will arise and shepherd His flock in the strength of the Lord, in the majesty of the name of the Lord His God. And they will remain, because at that time He will be great to the ends of the earth. And this One will be our peace."** (Micah 5:1-5 NASB) This passage tells us the Messiah will come from Bethlehem, inferring a human origin, but also states He will have existed from *eternity*, implying deity. Again, Philippians two tells us that Jesus pre-existed in the form of God and humbled Himself -- **taking the form of a bondservant, and being made in the likeness of men.** (Philippians 2:7)

THE prophets foretold that the Messiah would be born in Bethlehem, and ride into Jerusalem mounted on a donkey.

The prophet Zechariah wrote; **"Rejoice greatly, O daughter of Zion, shout in triumph, O daughter of Jerusalem! Behold your King is coming to you; He is just and endowed with salvation, humble and mounted on a donkey, even on a colt, the foal of a donkey"** (Zechariah 9:9 NASB). What an amazing prophecy. How absurd it was to predict a king would present himself on a donkey. A good guess would have been on a dashing white charger -- but not on a donkey!

Remember the comparison of a prediction and a prophecy: A prophecy is the telling ahead of time that something totally improbable will happen. No one, trying to make a good guess, would predict that the greatest of all kings would present Himself on a donkey. It is no accident that the One referred to as the King of Kings presented Himself to His people on the back of a donkey. It was part of God's plan. He was born in a manger, worked as a carpenter, presented Himself on a donkey, died between two criminals, and He is today, two thousand years after His death, recognized as the greatest leader and teacher the world has ever known. No, He was not merely an aberration of history. He was, and is, the Messiah sent by God to redeem us from our sin!

The prophetic twenty-second Psalm even describes in detail events surrounding the crucifixion of Jesus. It begins with the exact words Christ would later say on the cross, describes events that would take place around the cross, and then pictures Him in victory:

My God, my God, why have you forsaken me? ... O my God, I cry out by day, but you do not answer, by night, and am not silent. Yet you are enthroned as the Holy One; You are the praise of Israel. ... But I am a worm and not a man, scorned by men and despised by the people.

All who see me mock me; they hurl insults, shaking their heads: "He trusts in the Lord; let the Lord rescue him. Let him deliver him, since he delights in him." ... I am poured out like water, and all my bones are out of joint. My heart has turned to wax; it has melted away within me. My strength is dried up like a potsherd, and my tongue sticks to the roof of my mouth; you lay me in the dust of death.... a band of evil men has encircled me, they have pierced my hands and my feet. I can count all my bones; people stare and gloat over me. They divide my garments among them and cast lots for my clothing....

You who fear the Lord, praise him! All you descendants of Jacob, honor him! Revere him, all you descendants of Israel! ... All the ends of the earth will remember and turn to the Lord, and all the families of the nations will bow down before him, for dominion belongs to the Lord and he rules over the nations. (Psalm 22:1-28)

God Told Daniel <u>When</u> the Messiah Would Come

In the book of Daniel, we find one of the most amazing prophecies of all. Daniel was an Israelite who was living in Babylon during the Babylonian captivity. In the first part of chapter nine, Daniel makes one of the great prayers of the Bible. It was a prayer of true contrition for the sins of his nation, acknowledging that they were in captivity as a result of being disobedient to the Law given through Moses:

I prayed to the Lord my God and confessed: "O Lord, the great and awesome God, who keeps his covenant of love with all who love Him and obey his commands, we have sinned and done wrong. We have been wicked and have rebelled; we have turned away from your commands and laws. We have not listened to your servants the prophets, who spoke in your name to our kings, our princes and our fathers, and to all the people of the land. Lord, you are righteous, but this day we are covered with shame -- the men of Judah and people of Jerusalem and all Israel, both near and far, in all the countries where you have scattered us because of our unfaithfulness to you. O Lord, we and our kings, our princes and our fathers are covered with shame because we have sinned against you."

The Lord our God is merciful and forgiving, even though we have rebelled against him; we have not obeyed the Lord our God or kept the laws he gave us through his servants the prophets. All Israel has transgressed your law and turned away, refusing to obey you. Therefore the curses and sworn judgments written in the Law of Moses, the servant of God, have been poured out on us, because we have sinned against you. ... Just as it is written in the Law of Moses, all this disaster has come upon us, yet we have not sought the favor of the Lord our God by turning from our sins and giving attention to your truth. (Daniel 9:4-13)

In verses fifteen through nineteen, Daniel pleads with God to restore Jerusalem and God's Holy sanctuary; not for the sake of Israel, but for the sake of God's holy name. Verses twenty through twenty-three tell that God is about to answer Daniel's prayer by sending a message through Gabriel. This leads to four of the most important verses in the Old Testament prophets:

Seventy 'sevens' are decreed for your people and your holy city to finish transgression, to put an end to sin, to atone for wickedness, to bring in everlasting righteousness, to seal up vision and prophecy and to anoint the most holy. Know and understand this: From the issuing of the decree to restore and rebuild Jerusalem until the Anointed One (Messiah), the ruler, comes, there will be seven 'sevens,' and sixty-two 'sevens.' It will be rebuilt with streets and a trench, but in times of trouble.

After the sixty-two 'sevens,' the Anointed One will be cut off and will have nothing. The people of the ruler who will come will destroy the city and the sanctuary. The end will come like a flood: War will continue until the end, and desolations have been decreed. He will confirm a covenant with many for one 'seven.' In the middle of the 'seven' he will put an end to sacrifice and offering. And on a wing of the temple he will set up an abomination that causes desolation, until the end that is decreed is poured out on him. (Daniel 9:24-27)

Daniel lived around 500 B.C. There is a debate over when the Book of Daniel was written, but we know it was translated from Hebrew to Greek about 150 B.C. (as part of the first book ever translated from one language to another, the Septuagint). So we know this book was written several hundred years before Jesus was born. When examined closely, we find this prophecy in Daniel actually foretold when the Messiah would present himself. The starting and ending dates of this prophecy can be confirmed from Webster's dictionary or any good encyclopedia, so this prophecy deserves further examination:

Daniel chapter nine states that a total of seventy sevens are decreed upon Jerusalem "... to finish transgression, to put an end to sin, to atone for wickedness, to bring in everlasting righteousness, to seal up vision and prophecy and to anoint the most holy." But from the decree to rebuild Jerusalem unto the time of the coming of Messiah would be sixty-nine sevens (seven sevens plus sixty-two sevens).

The word translated *sevens* in the NIV translation is translated *weeks* in many other translations. In the Hebrew calendar there were weeks of days, but there were also weeks of years (every seven years they had a sabbatical rest year). The inference is that the city would be rebuilt in the first seven weeks, an impossibility if the time span was weeks of days. In Daniel 10:2 the word is used to refer to weeks of days, but there it is modified in the Hebrew language as "sevens of days." In chapter nine there is no such modifier. The Revised Standard Version correctly translates it **"seventy weeks of years"** and there is little doubt that the seventy sevens are weeks of years, not days. The calendar the Israelites used in those days was the Chaldean Calendar that had three hundred and sixty days in a year. So sixty-nine weeks of seven years each, with each year having three hundred sixty days, equals 173,880 days. (69 X 7 X 360 = 173,880).

Notice that the clock started at the time of the announcement to rebuild Jerusalem. There is only one such announcement found in the Bible. It is found in Nehemiah 2:1-7, and is precisely dated:

In the month of Nisan in the twentieth year of King Artaxerxes, when wine was brought for him, I took the wine and gave it to the king. I had not been sad in his presence before; so the king asked me, "Why does your face look so sad when you are not ill? This can be nothing but sadness of heart." I was very much afraid, but I said to the king, "May the king live forever! Why should my face not look sad when the city where my fathers are buried lies in ruins, and its gates have been destroyed by fire?" The king said to me, "What is it you want?" Then I prayed to the God of heaven, and I answered the king, "If it pleases the king and if your servant has found favor in his sight, let him send me to the city in Judah where my fathers are buried so that I can rebuild it."

Then the king, with the queen sitting beside him, asked me, "How long will your journey take, and when will you get back?" It pleased the king to send me; so I set a time. I also said to him, "If it pleases the king, may I have letters to the governors of Trans-Euphrates, so that they will provide me safe conduct until I arrive in Judah?"

You can check any dictionary with a biographical names section, and you will find the dates of Artaxerxes' reign. Merriam Webster's Collegiate Dictionary (Tenth Edition, page 1398) has the following information about Artaxerxes:

Artaxerxes, name of three Persian kings;
Artaxerxes I died 425 B.C. (reigned 465-25)

The first King Artaxerxes was the Artaxerxes living during the time of the Babylonian Captivity. His reign began in 465 B.C., and the announcement was made during the twentieth year of his reign. Since it was *during* the twentieth year, it was made in 445 B.C. (You subtract instead of add during B.C.) Beginning from the date of the order to rebuild Jerusalem, 173,880 days later would be the time prophesied for the coming of **"Anointed One** (Messiah) **the ruler."** The 173,880 days need to be converted to our Julian calendar, so we divide the 173,880 by 365.25 and come up with 475 of our calendar years. Subtracting the 444 years (from 445 B.C. to 1 B.C. = 444 years) leaves 32 years. While there is a debate among Bible scholars about the *exact* date, the year for the coming of **"Messiah the prince"** (Daniel 9:25 KJV) computes out to 31 or 32 A.D.

Luke 3:1 records that Jesus' ministry began "**... in the fifteenth year of the reign of Tiberius Caesar.**" Again turning to Webster, we learn that the reign of Tiberius began in July of 14 A.D. The fifteenth year would begin in July of 28 and last through June of 29 A.D. Add three years for the ministry of Jesus, and you arrive at the spring of 32 A.D., the time of the end of Jesus Christ's ministry here on earth. The math going from B.C. to A.D. is a little tricky, but there is no doubt that the sixty-nine weeks of years prophesied in Daniel culminated during the latter part of Jesus Christ's visitation to planet earth.

Daniel 9:26 tells us that after the sixty-nine sevens, Messiah will be *cut off*. Jesus was *cut off* by crucifixion at the end of His earthly ministry. (We will look at the seventieth week later in this book.) The prophecy also foretold that Jerusalem would be destroyed after the Messiah was cut off. This happened in seventy A.D. when the Romans, led by Titus, devastated Jerusalem.

This prophecy from Daniel is truly amazing. It not only tells us when the Messiah would present Himself, but that after Messiah presented Himself, He would be cut off, and that still later Jerusalem would be destroyed! The timing and sequence of the events are exact, and the starting and ending dates of the prophecy can be confirmed within one year from a dictionary or an encyclopedia (books not written with any significant bias).

Over 100 years ago, Sir Robert Anderson wrote a book entitled The Coming Prince (Reprint, Grand Rapids, Kregel 1963). Anderson was the head of Scotland Yard in England, and was noted for his work as a master detective. He was also an outstanding Bible scholar. In his research he asked the Astronomer Royal (an official in England) to precisely date the starting and ending dates of this prophecy. The conclusion of the Astronomer Royal was that the ending date was the exact date of the original Palm Sunday. Read Luke's description of the events of that day:

He sent two of his disciples, saying, "Go into the village opposite you, in which as you enter you will find a colt tied, on which no one has ever sat; untie it and bring it here. And if anyone asks you, 'Why are you untying it?' thus shall you speak, 'The Lord has need of it.'" And those who were sent went away and found it just as He had told them. And as they were untying the colt, its owners said to them, "Why are you untying the colt?" And they said, "The Lord has need of it."

And they brought it to Jesus, and they threw their garments on the colt and put Jesus on it. And as He was going, they were spreading their garments in the road. And as He was now approaching, near the descent of the Mount of Olives, the whole multitude of disciples began to praise God joyfully with a loud voice for all the miracles which they had seen, saying, "Blessed is the King who comes in the name of the Lord!" "Peace in heaven and glory in the highest!" And some of the Pharisees in the crowd said to Him, "Teacher, rebuke Your disciples!" And He answered and said "I tell you, if these become silent, the stones will cry out."

And when He approached, He saw the city and wept over it saying, "If you had only known in this day, even you, the things which make for perfect peace! But now they have been hidden from your eyes. For the days shall come upon you when your enemies will throw up a bank against you, and surround you, and hem you in on every side, and will level you to the ground, and your children within you, and they will not

leave in you one stone upon another, because you did not recognize the time of your visitation." (Luke 19:29-44)

The original Palm Sunday was Jesus' formal offering of
Himself as Messiah to Israel. As Jesus entered Jerusalem, the
people joyfully shouted, **"Blessed is the king who comes in the
name of the Lord."** These words were from the 118th Psalm and
were to be proclaimed when the Messiah arrived. The Pharisees,
recognizing the significance of this event, asked Jesus to rebuke
the disciples (who were waving boughs as commanded in the
Psalm). They also knew that when Jesus got on the donkey He
was presenting Himself as Messiah, as foretold in Zechariah 9:9,
but they were afraid to challenge Him personally.

Rather than rebuking His disciples, Jesus replied to the
Pharisees, **"I tell you, if these become silent, the stones will cry
out."** Then He told them the city (Jerusalem) would be
destroyed, which it was in seventy A.D. (about thirty-eight years
later). This also brings to mind the words of Jesus in Matthew
23:37-39:

**O Jerusalem, Jerusalem, who kills the prophets and stones
those sent to her! How often I wanted to gather your children
together, the way a hen gathers her chicks under her wings,
but you were unwilling. Behold, your house is being left to you
desolate. For I say to you, from now on you shall not see Me
until you say, "Blessed is He who comes in the name of the
Lord."**

DANIEL'S PROPHECY FORETOLD WHEN MESSIAH WAS GOING TO VISIT
EARTH. THE STARTING AND ENDING DATES OF THIS PROPHECY CAN
BE CONFIRMED WITHIN ONE YEAR FROM THE BEGINNING DATES OF THE
REIGNS OF RULERS GIVEN IN WEBSTER'S DICTIONARY.

Some years ago a Jewish rabbi, named Dr. Hugh J.
Schoenfeld, wrote a book entitled The Passover Plot (New York,
NY, Random House, 1965) to try to explain away the Messianic
claims of Jesus. As a scholar, Dr. Schoenfeld could not deny the
evidence that clearly establishes that thousands of Israelites in

the first century believed Jesus had risen from the grave and that He was the Messiah. As one who rejected any possibility of super-naturalism, and had negative emotional feelings toward Christianity (both obvious from the introduction to the book), Schoenfeld had to find an explanation for this phenomenon.

His explanation was that Jesus had set out to fulfill the Old Testament prophecies, but that He really did not die on the cross, rather, He merely went into a coma. He gave a variation of what is called the "swoon theory." Schoenfeld's explanation of why so many first century Jews believed Jesus was the Messiah is interesting. It included that Jesus was a great leader and teacher, and that He came to earth at the precise time when the prophet Daniel predicted the Messiah would arrive.

The book is utterly amazing. Schoenfeld establishes that Jesus fulfilled all of the requirements to be the Messiah, includ-ing *being born in the right town,* and *living at the right time* in history. Then he turns 180 degrees and concludes that Jesus was not the Messiah. He gives no further explanation why he rejects Jesus' messianic claims. He just blindly rejects. It is noteworthy that Dr. Schoenfeld offered no alternative person to Jesus, even though he recognized that the book of Daniel had prophesied the Messiah would visit earth during that era. The obvious question is: "If not Jesus, then what other person from that era could be the Messiah?"

Old Testament prophecies seemed to describe two Messiahs. They actually pointed to one Messiah coming two times!

It has often been observed that some of the prophecies about the coming Messiah *seem to be* contradictory. Some pre-sent the Messiah as a future ruling king. But Daniel foretold He would be cut off. Some passages say men will bow their knees to Him, but Isaiah fifty-three described Him as the suffering Savior who would be despised and rejected by men. It is said that some of the rabbis who lived before the life of Christ, recognized these contradictions and concluded there would be two Messiahs. Today it is easy to see that the Old Testament prophets were not talking about two Messiahs, but rather, about <u>one</u> Messiah who would come <u>two different times</u>. First, He came as the suffering Savior -- a Man of sorrows who was cut off from His people. But, the tomb is empty, and after His resurrection Jesus promised to return to the earth in the future as the King of Kings.

The Rejection of the Messiah was Foretold

A natural question to ask is, "If the evidence was so strong, why did the Israelites reject Jesus as the Messiah?" The apostle Paul, who personally proclaimed these prophecies to many Jews, explains that there is a veil over their eyes (II Corinthians 3:15). The Psalmist foretold, **"The stone which the builders rejected has become the chief cornerstone"** (Psalm 118:22 and quoted in Acts 4:11). It could be added; *they were just being consistent.* As Stephen pointed out, they had rejected and stoned their prophets, and when the Messiah came, they crucified Him! (Acts 7:52). In a previous chapter, we looked at Isaiah 53:3 (in a Jewish translation), where it described the coming Messiah as: **"He was despised and rejected ... and we esteemed Him not."**

The rejection of the Messiah, and the setting aside of Israel for a period of time without a king, was also dramatically pictured by the Old Testament prophet, Hosea. Hosea married a woman named Gomer. Gomer's first child was from Hosea. She then had two additional children of harlotry. She finally sunk to half the value of a slave and was put on the auction block. It is obvious when one reads the entire book of Hosea, that it uses Hosea's marriage to symbolically depict the relationship between Israel and God. The unfaithfulness of Hosea's wife, Gomer, is a picture of the unfaithfulness of Israel to God -- Israel's idolatry. In describing the people of Israel, the prophet charges, **"My people consult their wooden idol, and their diviner's wand informs them; For a spirit of harlotry has led them astray, and they have played the harlot, departing from their God"** (Hosea 4:12 NASB).

The third chapter of Hosea tells us what happened at the auction: **The Lord said to me, "Go, show your love to your wife again, though she is loved by another and is an adulteress. Love her as the Lord loves the Israelites, though they turn to other gods and love the sacred raisin cakes." So I bought her** for fifteen shekels of silver and about a homer and a lethek of barley. (Half the value of a normal slave.) Then I told her, "You are to live with me many days; you must not be a prostitute or be intimate with any man, and I will live with you." For the Israelites will live many days without king or prince, without sacrifice or sacred stones, without ephod or idol. Afterward the Israelites will return and seek the Lord their God and David their king. They will come trembling to the Lord and to His blessings in the last days. (Hosea 3:1-5)

This short chapter paints a beautiful *before and after* analogy. Before the auction, Gomer was a harlot. Her husband bought her back. After buying her back she was purified.

The chapter ends with Hosea using his marriage to deliver a powerful prophetic message about the Israelites: "**For the Israelites will live many days without king or prince (rulers), without sacrifice or sacred stones** (where they worshiped false gods, see Hosea 10:1-2), **without ephod** (a garment worn by the priests) **or idol many days.**" This verse is remarkable. *Before* the purchase of Israel (by Christ's death on the cross), Israel had kings and rulers. They had a sacrificial system, though they abused it by worshiping false gods of wood and stone. The Levites served as priests for the nation, and as mentioned over and over again in the Old Testament, the children of Israel worshiped false gods like the gold calf and the false gods of the nations around them.

This amazing prophecy foretells that *after* the *purchase*, <u>all</u> of this would change. Israel would no longer have a king or rulers, the sacrifices would cease, the priesthood would be abandoned, and idolatry would <u>stop</u>. It was a prophecy of a dramatic change in national conditions and behavior. Later, He added, "**they will be wanderers among the nations**" (9:17).

Hosea's prophecy accurately pictures the nature of Israel today. Since being purchased, Israel has continued many days without an earthly king, the offering of sacrifices ceased when Israel lost the temple site in 70 A.D., and the Levitical priesthood has disappeared (Christ is now the High Priest). Finally, as the Israelites have wandered among the nations of the world, they have become staunchly monotheistic.

The prophecy of this dramatic change of behavior, from idolatry to monotheism, *was totally improbable,* particularly when one considers that it was the other nations who had previously enticed the Israelites into idolatry. It was like predicting that a man who has a history of promiscuity and adultery would become faithful to his wife, even if he traveled alone for years, and every night he checked into a house of prostitution instead of a hotel.

The final verse in the chapter, **"Afterward the Israelites will return and seek the Lord their God and David their king. They will come trembling to the Lord and to His blessings in the last days,"** pictures how Israel will respond after the "many days," when Jesus, the Messiah, returns to earth. The reference to **"David their king,"** is obviously pointing to the promised Messiah, a descendent of David, since this prophecy was written several generations after King David's death.

Israel Will Look Upon the One They Pierced

Another profound prophecy is found in Zechariah. The context for this prophecy is set in Zechariah 10:8-10, at a time when Israel will be regathered back to the promised land: **"I will whistle for them to gather them together, for I have redeemed them; and they will be as numerous as they were before. When I scatter them among the peoples, they will remember Me in far countries, and with their children they will come back." (NASB)**

Then in Zechariah twelve, events that will take place at the time when Israel is regathered to the land are described:

This is the word of the Lord concerning Israel... "I am going to make Jerusalem a cup that sends all the surrounding peoples reeling. Judah will be besieged as well as Jerusalem. On that day, when all the nations of the earth are gathered against her, I will make Jerusalem an immovable rock for all the nations. All who try to move it will injure themselves."

"On that day I will strike every horse with panic and its rider with madness," declares the Lord. "I will keep a watchful eye over the house of Judah, but I will blind all the horses of the nations. Then the leaders of Judah will say in their hearts, 'The people of Jerusalem are strong, because the Lord Almighty is their God.' On that day I will make the leaders of

Judah like a firepot in a woodpile, like a flaming torch among sheaves. They will consume right and left all the surrounding peoples, but Jerusalem will remain intact in her place. The Lord will save the dwellings of Judah first, so that the honor of the house of David and of Jerusalem's inhabitants may not be greater than that of Judah. On that day the Lord will shield those who live in Jerusalem, so that the feeblest among them will be like David, and the house of David will be like God, like the Angel of the Lord going before them."

"On that day I will set out to destroy all the nations that attack Jerusalem. And I will pour out on the house of David and the inhabitants of Jerusalem a spirit of grace and supplication. *They will look on Me, the one they have pierced,* (italics supplied) and they will mourn for Him as one mourns for an only child, and grieve bitterly for Him as one grieves for a firstborn son." (Zechariah 12:1-10)

The Jews will look upon Him whom they have pierced.

The picture in Zechariah is of Israel back in the land after being regathered in the last days. The nations of the world will all be allied against Israel. Then it says **the Lord will defend the inhabitants of Jerusalem ... so they** (Israel) **will look upon Me whom they have pierced.** (NASB) This can only refer to Jesus. They pierced His hands and feet when they put Him on the cross!

A Closed Gate Stands Today as Solid Rock Evidence

There are many other Old Testament passages that give supporting evidence that Jesus was and is the Messiah. To keep this book short, there is room for just one more.

Then the man brought me to the gate facing east, and I saw the glory of the God of Israel coming from the east. His voice was like the roar of rushing waters, and the land was radiant with His glory. The vision I saw was like the vision I had seen when He came to destroy the city and like the visions I had seen by the Kebar River, and I fell facedown.

The glory of the Lord entered the temple through the gate facing east. (Ezekiel 43:1-4)

Then the man brought me back to the outer gate of the sanctuary, the one facing east, and it was shut. The Lord said to me, "This gate is to remain shut. It must not be opened; no one may enter through it. It is to remain shut because the Lord, the God of Israel, has entered through it. The prince himself is the only one who may sit inside the gateway to eat in the presence of the Lord. He is to enter by way of the portico of the gateway and go out the same way." (Ezekiel 44:1-2)

When Jesus entered Jerusalem to present Himself to Israel as their Messiah, on the original Palm Sunday, He descended from the Mount of Olives (Luke 19:37), and thus He entered Jerusalem though the Eastern Gate, referred to in these passages in Ezekiel. Ezekiel told us **"the glory of the Lord entered the temple through the gate facing east."** Then he prophesied, **"This gate is to remain shut. It must not be opened; no one may enter through it. It is to remain shut because the Lord, the God of Israel, has entered through it."**

Today, the Eastern Gate, also called the Golden Gate, is a solid stone wall within the ancient arches. It has been *shut*, and today no one enters by it. The stones and mortar that now fill that arch are rock solid evidence that the Lord God, Messiah, has already entered Jerusalem.

Tradition says that the Eastern Gate will not be opened again until the Messiah returns. When Kaiser Wilhelm II of Germany heard this, he announced that after he won the First World War, he was going to have that gate opened so that he could personally enter Jerusalem by it -- but he never made it through that gate! Today the gate still remains sealed, waiting for the return of Jesus the Messiah!

No One Living After 70 A.D. Can Qualify as the Messiah

One last thought before proceeding. As noted, the Messiah is to be a descendant of King David. Today, no one can establish they are a descendant of David. *The genealogies were all destroyed when Jerusalem was destroyed in 70 A.D.*

The genealogical records, that weave their way though the Old Testament, culminate in the books of Matthew and Luke with Jesus. Both His legal line through Joseph and His blood line through Mary are traced back to King David.

Either Jesus is the Messiah, or there will never be a Messiah, for the Messiah must be a descendant of King David, and He had to present Himself to Israel on or about the year 32 A.D. No one other than Jesus has fulfilled the Messianic prophecies. Furthermore, the door has been closed for all after Him.

If we were to dig in the newspapers of 1992, we could probably find a prediction that people were going to come from all over the world for a gigantic athletic event in Atlanta, Georgia in the summer of 1996. You're probably thinking, "That was not a prophecy. That was an announcement from the Olympic Committee about what they were going to hold the Olympic Games in Atlanta."

If the Olympic Committee announced what they were going to do four years in advance, is it a surprise that God announced what He was going to do several hundred years in advance? After all, the most important event in the history of the world surely deserved some advance notice!

A simple explanation for the why of biblical prophecy is that God announced ahead of time what He was going to do:

"But the things which God announced beforehand by the mouth of all the prophets, that His Christ (Messiah) **should suffer, He has thus fulfilled."** (Acts 3:18)

SUMMARY OF CHAPTER SEVEN:

After King David had conquered his enemies, God gave him a promise that a descendant of his would always reign as king of Israel. This promise, called the Davidic Covenant, is the foundation for the promises that One will come who is called the Messiah. The Old Testament prophets gave many specific details about the promised Messiah, but there seemed to be two diverse pictures of Him. Today we see these were not about two different Messiahs, rather, they describe one Messiah, Jesus Christ, who would come to this planet -- two different times.

CHAPTER 8
HE CAME UNTO HIS OWN, BUT ...

Take a mental journey back to the first century and picture yourself as a Jew living in Palestine. You know God has made promises to your people through Abraham. Your nation has been promised it will be given all of the land from the river of Egypt to the Euphrates River, and that through your nation all other nations in the world will be blessed. From reading your Bible (the Old Testament), you know that because of disobedience to the Law of Moses, your people went into captivity, some were later returned to the land, but many of your people are yet scattered around the world.

You also know that God made a promise that a descendant of King David would be Messiah. You have read the prophets of old as they repeatedly proclaimed: "He is coming!" "The Messiah is coming!" "The King is coming!" You long for His arrival because you are living in a nation dominated by a foreign power, the strongest power in the world of your day -- Rome. You would desperately like to see the Messiah come and deliver your people from bondage.

Now, let's take a look at what happened when the Messiah arrived. The book that provides a transition from the Old Testament to the New Testament is the Book of Matthew. We find the key to understanding Matthew in John, chapter one: **"He came unto His own, and His own received Him not. But as many as received Him, to them He gave power to become the sons of God, even to those who believe on His name"** (John 1:11-12 KJV).

The great Bible teacher, Donald Barnhouse, wrote a commentary on Matthew, and he titled it, *He Came Unto His Own, But*. It was an appropriate name because Matthew is the gospel that presents Jesus as the King offered to Israel, and that title, from John's gospel, sums up the main story of Matthew in a part of a sentence.

There are two verses, Matthew 4:17 (referring to the time beginning from Matthew 4:12) and Matthew 16:21, that both use the phrase **"From that time Jesus began to..."** These verses divide the book of Matthew into three main sections. These sections also serve as an outline that helps us understand the flow of the earthly life of Jesus:

    I. The Preparation for the King - Matthew 1:1 - 4:11
   II. The Presentation of the King - Matthew 4:12 - 16:20
  III. The Passing of the King - Matthew 16:21 - 28:20

The Preparation for the King

Matthew one records the genealogy of Jesus through His legal father Joseph, whereas Luke records His bloodline through Mary. These records establish Jesus' right to be Messiah, because He is both a legal and blood descendant of King David. The remainder of chapter one and chapter two, of Matthew, tell of events surrounding Jesus' birth. Chapter three tells of the ministry of John the Baptist and the baptism of Jesus. Matthew 4:1-11 tells of the temptation in the wilderness. We have given Matthew 1:1 through 4:11 the title: "The Preparation for the King."

The Presentation of the King

Beginning with Matthew 4:12 there is a shift. In verse seventeen of Matthew four, referring to the time beginning with verse twelve, Matthew tells us; **"From that time Jesus began to preach and say, 'Repent for the kingdom of heaven is at hand.'"** It is important to notice that prior to that time, Jesus did not preach, **"the kingdom of heaven is at hand."** Here, the phrase **"From that time Jesus began"** signals the shift to the second phase of Jesus' life. This same phrase will be used later, in Matthew, and these two uses of it are like hinges on which the three sections of Matthew's Gospel swing. We call the second section: "The Presentation of the King." It includes the offer and rejection of Jesus as Messiah.

Notice, Jesus proclaimed, "...the kingdom of heaven is at hand." The Greek expression translated *at hand* means it can come at any time. The Jews knew from their scriptures (the Old Testament) that for the kingdom to be established, the Messiah must come first. So when Jesus said, "...the kingdom of heaven is at hand," He was telling them that the coming of the Messiah was imminent -- He was at the door.

Jesus did not define the word *kingdom*, other than to imply that its source was from heaven. When Jesus was preaching **"the Gospel of the Kingdom,"** if He was not referring to the Kingdom foretold in the Old Testament, it would have been an imperative that He make a clear differentiation.

The word *Gospel* means "good news." There are many views as to exactly what is meant by the "Kingdom of Heaven" and/or the "Kingdom of God," and there may be different things implied when the terms are used in different contexts. Jesus' message here must have included that the kingdom God promised in the Old Testament could come at any time; therefore, the arrival of Messiah was near! To start out His ministry by stating that He was the Messiah would have been too abrupt. Later, when asked directly, He did affirm this claim (Jesus before Pilate in John eighteen). But first, Jesus needed to establish His credentials.

Matthew, chapters five through seven, records the Sermon on the Mount. We could describe the Sermon on the Mount as, "the constitution of the coming kingdom." It ends with the statement, **"The result was that when Jesus had finished these words, the multitudes were amazed at His teaching; for He was teaching them as one who having authority, and not as their scribes"** (Matthew 7:28-29). In the Sermon on the Mount, Jesus established His authority, and *thus who He was, by the words He spoke.* It should be added that, throughout His ministry, Jesus continued to establish who He was through words He spoke.

Matthew eight and nine, record that Jesus healed the sick, made the lame to walk, the blind to see, and cast out demons. Jesus established *who He was by the miracles He performed.*

JESUS ESTABLISHED WHO HE WAS BY THE WORDS
HE SPOKE, AND BY THE MIRACLES HE PERFORMED!

In Matthew ten, Jesus gathered a group of men, the twelve disciples, and sent them out with specific instructions:

These twelve Jesus sent out after instructing them, saying, "Do not go in the way of the Gentiles, and do not enter any city of the Samaritans; but rather got to the lost sheep of the house of Israel. And as you go, preach, saying, "The kingdom of heaven is at hand." Heal the sick, raise the dead, cleanse the lepers, cast out demons; freely you have received, freely give. Do not acquire gold or silver or copper for your money belts, or a bag for your journey, or even two tunics, or sandals or a staff; for the worker is worthy of his support.

And whatever town or village you enter, inquire who is worthy in it; and abide there until you go away. And as you enter the house, give it your greeting. And if the home is worthy, let your greeting of peace come upon it; but if it is not worthy, let your greeting of peace return to you. And whoever does not receive you or heed your words, as you go out of that house or city, shake off the dust of your feet. Truly I say to you, it will be more tolerable for the land of Sodom and Gomorrah in the day of judgment than for that city.

Behold, I send you out as sheep in the midst of wolves; therefore be as shrewd as serpents and innocent as doves. But beware of men; for they will deliver you up to the courts, and scourge you in their synagogues; and you shall even be brought before governors and kings for my sake, as a testimony to them and to the Gentiles. But they will deliver you up, do not become anxious about how or what you speak; for it shall be given you in that hour what you are to speak. For it is not you who speak, but it is the Spirit of your Father who speaks in you. And brother will deliver up another brother to death, and a father his child; and children will rise up against parents, and cause them to be put to death. And you will be hated by all because of My name, but it is the one who has endured to the end who will be saved. But whenever the persecute you in this city, flee to the next; for truly I say to you, you shall not finish going through the cities of Israel, until the Son of Man comes. (Matthew 10:5-23)

Notice that Jesus told them to not go to the Gentiles, but only to the **"lost sheep of the house of Israel."** (But, He also told them that their speaking to Israel would serve as a testimony to the Gentiles.) Later, Jesus told His disciples to go to the whole world. One might ask, "Isn't this a contradiction?" No, we need to understand the context. At this time, Jesus and His disciples were presenting Jesus as Messiah, but only to the nation of Israel. In the Abrahamic Covenant, God had promised that through the descendants of Abraham, all families of the earth would be blessed. Israel was to be the instrument God would use to minister to all mankind: But, the children of Israel needed to first accept Jesus as their Messiah -- so they could then minister to the world.

He also told His disciples not to take money and extra shoes. Today we do not always take extra shoes when we travel, but in those days they walked. In the context of offering Jesus as Messiah to Israel, apparently God made a supernatural provision for them just as He did for the children of Israel when they wandered in the wilderness -- their shoes did not wear out. This should not be taken out of its context. Jesus was not laying down a principle for future missionaries whom He would send to the nations of the world.

In Matthew 10:23, Jesus warned them that they should expect persecution, but that they would not finish the assignment **"before the Son of Man comes."** (The name **"the Son of Man"** was one of Jesus' favorite expressions for Himself.) This is another bit of evidence that He sent them out to present Him as Messiah, though the message may have been somewhat veiled at that time.

First Sign of Rejection -- John the Baptist Put in Prison

In Matthew eleven, John the Baptist, who had previously testified for Jesus, was put in prison. Apparently having doubts, John sent his disciples to Jesus to ask, **"Are you the Expected One, or shall we look for someone else?"** John's question indicated he wanted to know whether Jesus was the promised Messiah. Jesus answered beginning in verse four, **"Go and report to John what you hear and see: The blind receive sight, the lame walk, the lepers are cleansed and the deaf hear, and the dead are raised up, and the poor have the Gospel preached to them. And blessed is he who keeps from stumbling over Me"** (Matthew 11:4-6). We saw earlier that Jesus had established whom He was by both the words He spoke and the miracles He performed. His answer here can only be taken as an affirmative answer. In essence, Jesus replied, "Consider what I have *said* and *done*, and you will have your answer!"

In chapter eleven, Jesus' very language seems to change. Jesus was being criticized as **"a friend of tax collectors,"** and **"... He began to reproach the cities in which most of His miracles were done, because they did not repent."** As He reproached the cities, He made a profound statement that is recorded in Matthew 11:23-24:

And you, Capernaum, will not be exalted to heaven, will you? You shall descend to Hades; for if the miracles had occurred in Sodom which occurred in you, it would have remained to this day. Nevertheless I say to you that it shall be more tolerable for the land of Sodom in the day of judgment, than for you.

Now, Capernaum was not that bad when compared to Sodom. After all, Sodom was one of the most wicked cities in the ancient world -- the source of the word *sodomy*. The question arises, how could things be worse for Capernaum on the Judgment day than for Sodom? This passage teaches an important principle: The severity of judgment will have a relationship to the light that was given!

The most common objection to the Gospel one hears is, "What about the natives in Africa who have never heard it?" I once led a seminar that included a student from Africa. He said,

"In Africa the big question is -- What about the heathen in America who have never heard?" When we consider Jesus' words in Matthew eleven, we can't help but conclude that, on the judgment day, one would be better off as a native from the "bush" who had *never* heard the Gospel, than as a privileged citizen of the United States who had heard the Gospel over and over again, and still *rejected* the light that was given!

SINCE God's judGMENT will CONSidER THE liGHT THAT WAS GivEN, iT follows THAT ONE would bE bETTER off ON THE judGMENT dAy TO bE A NATivE fROM "THE bush" who HAd NEVER hEARd of JESUS, THAN TO bE SOMEONE who HAd HEARd THE GOSPEL, buT HAd REjECTEd God's offER of REdEMPTiON!

A paraphrase of Jesus' words could say, **"It will be more tolerable for the land of Sodom in the day of judgment than for anyone who has heard the Gospel and rejected or ignored it."** Jesus elsewhere expressed the same principle when He said, **"To those who much is given, much will be required"** (Luke 12:48). As one of my favorite professors often commented: *"A word to the wise should be sufficient."*

Matthew eleven records the first signs that Israel is rejecting Jesus as Messiah. This rejection accelerates in the following chapters. In chapter twelve, the Pharisees accused Jesus of doing His miracles by the power of Satan. In chapter thirteen, Jesus begins using parables. His disciples ask why. Read His response:

And He answered and said to them, "To you it has been granted to know the mysteries of the kingdom of heaven, but to them it has not been granted. For whoever has, to him shall more be given, and he shall have an abundance; but whoever does not have, even what he has will be taken away from him. Therefore I speak to them in parables; because while seeing, they do not see, and while hearing, they do not hear nor do they understand. And in their case the prophecy of Isaiah is being fulfilled, which says;

Your eyes keep on hearing but will not understand;
And you will keep on seeing, but will not perceive;
For the heart of this people has become dull, and
    with their ears they scarcely hear,
And they have closed their eyes
Lest they should see with their eyes,
And hear with their ears,
And understand with their heart and return,
And I should heal them.

"But blessed are your eyes, because they see, and your ears, because they hear. For truly I say to you, that many prophets and righteous men desired to see what you see, and did not see it, and to hear what you hear, and did not hear it." (Matthew 13:11-17)

Jesus adopted the parabolic method of teaching so He could continue to teach truth to those with the right heart attitude and hide it from those with a wrong, rejecting attitude. That He had to resort to this method was another sign of mounting rejection by the leaders of Israel.

The Report Card at Caesarea Philippi

Jesus continues to teach and heal in the next few chapters. Matthew sixteen, another key chapter, contains the second use of the phrase, **"from that time Jesus began."** As mentioned earlier, these two uses of the same phrase serve like *hinges* on which the three sections of the book of Matthew swing. Read the text from Matthew 16:13-20:

Now when Jesus came into the district of Caesarea Philippi, He began asking His disciples, saying, "Who do people say that the Son of Man is?" And they said, "Some say John the Baptist; and others, Elijah; but still others, Jeremiah, or one of the prophets." "He said to them, "But who do you say that I am?" And Simon Peter answered and said, "Thou art the Christ, the Son of the living God."

And Jesus answered and said to him, "Blessed are you, Simon Barjona, because flesh and blood did not reveal this to you, but My Father who is in heaven. And I also say to you that you are Peter, and upon this rock I will build My church, and the gates of Hades shall not overcome it. I will give you the keys of the kingdom of heaven; whatever you shall bind on earth shall be bound in heaven, and whatever you shall loose on earth shall be loosed in heaven." Then He warned the disciples that they should tell no one that He was the Christ.

This passage could be called the mid-term report card time for Israel. Jesus had been establishing who He was by the words He spoke and the miracles He performed. He had sent out his disciples preaching the **"Gospel of the Kingdom."** He had established that He was the Messiah. He gathers His disciples back together and asks them **"Who do people say the Son of Man is?"** (He often used *The Son of Man* to refer to Himself.)

In their answer, the important response was not *whom they were willing to say He was!* What was important was w*hom they were NOT willing to say He was!* Oh yes, they were willing to say that maybe He was a reincarnated prophet, but the Israelites were NOT willing to say Jesus was the Messiah. Their answer indicated that the Israelites were rejecting the offer of Jesus as their Messiah. As John 1:11 said, **"He came unto His own, but His own received Him not!"**

The Jews were NOT willing to say, "Jesus is the Messiah!"

Then Jesus turned to His disciples and asked, **"But who do you say that I am?"** Peter responded with that great affirmation, **"You art the Christ,** (which means the Anointed One or the Messiah) **the Son of the Living God."** Notice Jesus did not rebuke Peter for his answer, rather He said Peter was blessed as a result of making that affirmation. He then announced a major undertaking when He said, **"I will build MY church."**

At that time, Jesus did *not* say, "I am NOW building my church." He used the future tense. Jesus did not establish His church until after His resurrection. It was something new. Paul later described it as a mystery, and the Greek word translated *mystery* meant something that had not previously been revealed. His church-building ministry was not initiated prior to His rejection by Israel.

The Passing of the King

Then Jesus did a surprising thing, **"... He warned the disciples that they should tell no one that He was the Christ."** Again we could ask, "Is not this a contradiction? Didn't Jesus command His disciples to tell everyone He is the Christ? What is going on here?" Verse twenty-one sets the context so we can understand this command. It contains the second usage of the "hinge phrase" in the book of Matthew:

From that time on Jesus Christ began **to show His disciples that He must go to Jerusalem, and suffer many things from the elders and chief priests and scribes, and be killed, and be raised up on the third day.** (Matthew 16:21).

Matthew 1:1 to 4:11 records "The Preparation for the King." In Matthew 4:12 through 16:20, Matthew told of "The Presentation (offering and rejection) of the King." Matthew 16:21 begins the final section of His gospel that goes through the end of the book and could be called, "The Passing of the King." So, as noted earlier, the earthly life of Jesus, the Messiah, can be divided into three parts:

I. The Preparation for the King - Matthew 1:1 - 4:11
II. The Presentation of the King - Matthew 4:12 - 16:20
III. The Passing of the King - Matthew 16:20 - 28:20

Prior to Matthew sixteen, Jesus directed most of His ministry to the large groups: The Sermon on the Mount, the feeding of the five thousand, and numerous other times when He ministered to the masses. From here on, Jesus concentrated on ministering to His disciples in small groups. Beginning in chapter sixteen, Jesus is preparing them for the job He announced in His response to Peter when He said, **"I will build My church."**

Just as the prophet Zechariah had prophesied, Jesus presented Himself as Messiah to Israel on the back of a donkey. This event, recorded in Matthew twenty-one, was the original Palm Sunday. When Jesus came into the city on that donkey, the people waved palm branches and shouted, **"Blessed is He who comes in the name of the Lord"** (Psalm 118:26). It is clear from their response, the leaders of Israel understood His disciples were proclaiming Him as Messiah, and that He encouraged and accepted their proclamation. The reaction of the leaders of Israel can only be described as negative.

On Palm Sunday, the leaders of Israel understood that His disciples were proclaiming Him as Messiah, and that Jesus accepted their proclamation.

In Matthew, chapters twenty-one and twenty-two, Jesus told two parables that help put the pieces together:

"A certain landowner planted a vineyard, built a wall around it, dug a pit for pressing out grape juice, and built a lookout tower. Then he leased the vineyard to tenant farmers and moved to another country. At the time of the grape harvest he sent his agents to collect his share of the crop. But the farmers grabbed his servants, beat one, killed one and killed another. So the landowner sent a larger group of his servants to collect for him, but the results were the same.

Finally the owner sent his son, thinking, "Surely they will respect my son."

But when the farmers saw the son coming, they said to one another, 'Here comes the heir to this estate. Come on, let's kill him and get the estate for ourselves!' So they grabbed him, took him out of the vineyard and murdered him.

"When the owner of the farm returns," Jesus asked, "What do you think he will do to those farmers?"

The religious leaders replied, "He will put the wicked men to a horrible death, and lease the vineyard to others who will give him his share of the crop after each harvest."

Then Jesus asked them, "Didn't you ever read this in the Scriptures: 'The stone rejected by the builders has become the cornerstone. This is the Lord's doing and it is marvelous to see.'

What I mean is that the kingdom of God will be taken away from you, and given to a nation that will produce the proper fruit. Anyone who stumbles over that stone will be broken to pieces, and it will crush anyone one on whom it falls."

When the leading priests and Pharisees heard Jesus, they realized he was pointing at them -- that they were the farmers in his story. They wanted to arrest Him, but were afraid to try because of the crowds considered Jesus a prophet. (Matthew 21:33-46 NLT)

The rejection was growing. There is no doubt that Jesus felt the animosity of the Jewish leaders, but He did not back off. He continued on with another parable:

"The Kingdom of Heaven can be illustrated by the story of a king who prepared a great wedding feast for his son. Many guests were invited, and when the banquet was ready he sent his servants to notify everyone that it was time to come. But they all refused! So he sent other servants to tell them, "The feast has been prepared, the choice meats have been cooked. Everything is ready. Hurry!" But the guests he had invited ignored them, and went about their business, one to his farm, another to his store. Others seized his messengers and treated them shamefully, even killing some of them.

Then the king became furious. He sent out his army to destroy the murderers and burn their city. And he said to his servants, 'The wedding feast is ready, and the guests I invited aren't worthy of the honor. Now go out to the street corners and invite everyone you see.'

So the servants brought in everyone they could find, good and bad alike, and the banquet hall was filled with guests. But when the king came in to meet the guests he noticed a man who wasn't wearing the proper clothes for a wedding. 'Friend,' he asked, 'How is it that you are here without a wedding clothes?' And the man had no reply. Then the king said to his aides, 'Bind him hand and foot and throw him out into the outer darkness where there is weeping and gnashing of teeth.' For many are called, but few are chosen."

Then the Pharisees met together to think of a way to trap Jesus into saying something for which they could accuse Him. (Matthew 22:2-15 NLT).

Both of these parables picture the rejection of Jesus as Messiah. The first needs no explanation. For sure, the Pharisees instantly caught what Jesus was saying.

The second parable is more complex. In it the king represents God the Father, and the son represents Jesus, the Son of God. The servants that went out the first time represent the disciples during Christ's earthly ministry. The rejection by those invited to the banquet represents the rejection by **"the lost sheep of Israel."** In this parable, servants were sent out a second time. This is a reference to what later happened during the time covered by the book of Acts and thereafter. Notice the response of some of the invited guests; they **"... seized his messengers and treated them shamefully, even killing some of them."** Then the King sent his army and destroyed their city. These things all happened, including the destruction of Jerusalem, in seventy A.D.

Then the slaves went out and **"brought in everyone they could find, good and bad alike; and the banquet hall was filled with guests."** One can surmise that in the parable the "bad" represented Gentiles and the "good" represented Jews. The Marriage Supper of the Lamb, a future event described in the book of Revelation, chapter nineteen, will be attended by people from **"all families of the world."** Jesus' offer of redemption is available to both Jews and Gentiles. He said, **"Come unto Me all you who are burdened, and I will give you rest"** (Matthew 11:28).

There is a real nugget in the last part of this parable. After the marriage of one of his daughters, a friend of mine commented: "I can identify with that guy in John chapter two. They ran out of wine -- because he ran out of money!" My friend should have realized things could have been worse. In this parable, the king not only paid for all of the dresses for the bridesmaids, he provided clothing for every guest at the wedding.

This is a picture of the Gospel. The clothes represent the righteousness that God provides for us through Christ. When we go to the "Marriage Supper of the Lamb," we must be covered by the righteousness of Jesus that is imputed to every believer. Anyone who tries to enter wearing his own clothing (his own claim of goodness) will be ejected, just as in the parable. Again, "*A word to the wise should be sufficient.*"

The Ultimate Prophecy About the Messiah is Fulfilled!

Notice the response of the Pharisees to this parable: **"Then the Pharisees went and counseled together how they might trap Him in what He said."** (Matthew 22:15). The rest of the story of Matthew is well known. They had Jesus crucified -- because He claimed to be the "King of Israel." Isaiah 53:10 (KJV) had foretold what would happen, **"... when thou shalt make His soul as an offering for sin ... He shall prolong His days, and the pleasure of the Lord shall proper in His hand."**

When Jesus died on the cross, He died as the Lamb of God -- a sacrifice for our sin. But, death could not hold Him. On Easter Sunday morning, He arose victorious from that tomb! For Jesus was a descendant of David, the Holy One of Israel, the promised Messiah, the Prince of Peace, and the King of Kings. No wonder the Christian world celebrates His resurrection by singing Handel's <u>Messiah</u>, with the triumphant Hallelujah Chorus. Yes --

He is risen! He is risen indeed!

Summary of Chapter Eight:

The Book of Matthew is the Gospel that best connects the New Testament to the Old Testament. It is the Gospel that presents Jesus Christ as the Messiah, the King of the Jews. In Matthew, we can see that the life of Christ had three phases: The Preparation for the King, The Presentation of the King, and The Passing of the King.

During the second phase, Jesus first established who He was by the words He spoke and the miracles He performed. He and His disciples proclaimed "the Gospel of the Kingdom." The king of that kingdom was to be the promised Messiah, whose arrival was imminent. The Jews knew that for the Kingdom promised in the Old Testament to come, the Messiah would have to come. Thus Jesus was being offered to Israel as Messiah.

The response of Israel was rejection. Finally, Jesus gathered His disciples and asked, "Who do men say I am?" The response indicated that the leaders of Israel were rejecting Him as Messiah. So Jesus turned to them and asked, "Who do you say I am?" Peter answered for the group and proclaimed Him as the Messiah. Jesus affirmed this belief and announced that, in the future, He would build His church.

Having been rejected, the final phase of Jesus' life here on earth focused on preparing His disciples for the task before them. He was formally presented to Israel, as Messiah, on Palm Sunday. He gave parables about His being rejected by the leaders of Israel, which precipitated their having Him crucified. But, the tomb could not hold Him and He rose victorious on Easter morning, for He is Lord of Lords and King of Kings. Hallelujah!

The Resurrection of Jesus - Fact or Fiction

It is not within the scope of this book to examine the evidence for the resurrection of Jesus Christ. If a reader still has doubts about the deity of Jesus Christ, an honest examination of that evidence should be undertaken.

When Simon Greenleaf, a professor of law at Harvard University and the author of The Principles of Legal Evidence, was challenged by some of his students to examine the evidence for the resurrection of Jesus, as it would be examined if tested in a court of law, he accepted their challenge. After he completed his examination of the evidence, Greenleaf concluded there is well-documented historical evidence for it, and added, "I am convinced that you could convince any jury in England or America that Jesus Christ rose from the dead."

Reference: Greenleaf, Simon. The Testimony of the Evangelist Examined by the Rules of Evidence Administered in the Courts of Justice. London 1874. Reprint, Grand Rapids, MI: Baker

CHAPTER 9
IT'S SOMETHING NEW

As mentioned in the introduction, as we move progressively through the Bible, there are times when it is like putting together a jigsaw puzzle. Before going on to the book of Acts and the New Testament epistles, we again need to put some *borders* in place so that we can properly understand how other parts fit in the big picture. The *borders* include a major Old Testament covenant that sets the stage for the remainder of the Bible. In the Old Testament, this covenant was prophetic (to be established in the future), so we delayed our examination of it until this place in our journey through the Scriptures. Jeremiah calls it the New Covenant.

Jeremiah, "the weeping prophet," wrote his prophecies just before the downfall of Jerusalem and the Babylonian captivity. We find the New Covenant in Jeremiah thirty-one, but we first need to look at a passage in chapter thirty-two to understand the historical context.

Then the word of the Lord came to Jeremiah: "I am the Lord, the God of all mankind. Is anything too hard for me?" Therefore, this is what the Lord says: "I am about to hand this city over to the Babylonians and to Nebuchadnezzar king of Babylon, who will capture it. The Babylonians who are attacking this city will come in and set it on fire; they will burn it down, along with the houses where the people provoked me to anger by burning incense on the roofs to Baal and by pouring out drink offerings to other gods. *The people of Israel and Judah have done nothing but evil in my*

sight from their youth; indeed, the people of Israel have done nothing but provoke me with what their hands have made, declares the Lord." (Jeremiah 32:26 - 30, italics supplied)

It is clear from this passage that the nation was in decline as a result of its sin and rebellion. However, even as the dark clouds of judgment gathered, God promised future blessings for Israel. With this background in mind, read Jeremiah's prophecy of the New Covenant in chapter thirty-one:

"Behold, days are coming," declares the Lord, "when I will make a new covenant with the house of Israel and with the house of Judah, not like the covenant which I made with their fathers, in the day that I took them by the hand to bring them out of the land of Egypt, my covenant which they broke, although I was a husband to them," declares the Lord.

"But this is the covenant which I will make with the house of Israel after those days," declares the Lord; "I will put My law within them and on their heart I will write it: and I will be their God and they shall be my people. And they shall not teach again, each man his neighbor and each man his brother, saying, 'Know the Lord,' for they shall all know me, from the least of them to the greatest of them," declares the Lord, "for I will forgive their iniquity, and their sin I will remember no more."

Thus says the Lord, who gives the sun for light by day, and the fixed order of the moon and the stars for light by night. Who stirs up the sea so that its waves roar; the Lord of hosts is his name: "If this fixed order departs from before me," declares the Lord, then the offspring of Israel also shall cease from being a nation before me forever." Thus says the Lord, "If the heavens above can be measured, and the foundations of the earth searched out below, (which they can't) then I will also cast off all the offspring of Israel for all that they have done," declares the Lord. "Behold, days are coming," declares the Lord, "when the city shall be rebuilt for the Lord from the Tower of Hananel to the Corner Gate ... it shall not be plucked up, or overthrown any more forever." (Jeremiah 31:31-40)

To those who would listen amidst their suffering, these promises from God were like a lifeline to which they could cling. But, most of the Israelites ignored Jeremiah's prophecy and were taken captive to Babylon. But, in spite of the judgment being fulfilled, the promise remained: The New Covenant would still be established sometime in the future. The promise was never revoked -- "**... for the gifts and the calling of God are irrevocable**" (Romans 11:29).

After Jeremiah's prophecy, the Southern Kingdom was taken captive to Babylon. While they were in Babylon, God raised up the prophet Ezekiel, and through Ezekiel, God gave another promise for the future that parallels the prophecy in Jeremiah. While Ezekiel does not call it the New Covenant, it is pretty clear both Jeremiah and Ezekiel were speaking about the same thing. Read that message to Israel in Ezekiel, chapter thirty-six:

Then the word of the Lord came to me saying, "Son of man, when the house of Israel was living in their own land, they defiled it by their ways and their deeds. ... Therefore, I poured out my wrath on them for the blood which they had shed on the land, because they had defiled it with their idols. Also I scattered them among the nations, and they were dispersed throughout the lands. According to their ways and their deeds I judged them. When they came to the nations where they went, they profaned my holy name, because it was said of them 'These are the people of the Lord; yet they have come out of His land.' But I had concern for my holy name, which the house of Israel had profaned among the nations where they went."

Therefore, say to the house of Israel, "Thus says the Lord God, 'It is not for your sake, O house of Israel, that I am about to act, but for My holy name, which you have profaned among the nations where you went. And I will vindicate the holiness of my great name which has been profaned among the nations, which you have profaned in their midst. Then the nations will know that I am the Lord,' declares the Lord, 'when I prove myself holy among you in their sight.

For I will take you from the nations, gather you from all the lands, and bring you into your own land. Then I will

sprinkle clean water on you, and you will be clean; I will cleanse you from all your filthiness and from all your idols. Moreover, I will give you a new heart and put a new spirit within you; and I will remove the heart of stone from your flesh and give you a heart of flesh. And I will put my Spirit within you and cause you to walk in my statutes, and you will be careful to observe my ordinances. And you will live in the land that I gave to your fathers; so you will be my people, and I will be your God.

Moreover, I will save you from all your uncleanness; and I will call for the grain and multiply it, and I will not bring a famine on you. And I will multiply the fruit of the tree and the produce of the field, that you may not receive again the disgrace of famine among the nations. Then you will remember your evil ways and your deeds that were not good, and you will loathe yourselves in your own sight for your iniquities and your abominations. I am not doing this for your sake,' declares the Lord God, 'let it be known to you. Be ashamed and confounded for your ways, O house of Israel!'"

Thus says the Lord God, "On the day when I cleanse you from all your iniquities, I will cause the cities to be inhabited and the waste places to be rebuilt. And the desolate land will be cultivated instead of being a desolation in the sight of everyone who passed by. And they will say, 'This desolate land has become like the garden of Eden; and the waste, desolate, and ruined cities are fortified and inhabited.' Then the nations that are left round about you will know that I, the Lord, have rebuilt the ruined places and planted that which was desolate; I, the Lord, have spoken and will do it." (Ezekiel 36:16-36)

The New Covenant was Established by Christ's Death on the Cross

Hebrews eight quotes Jeremiah's passage about the New Covenant. Then chapter nine tells us that the New Covenant was established by Christ's death on the cross:

But when Christ appeared as a high priest of the good things to come, He entered through the greater and more perfect tabernacle, not made with hands, that is to say, not of this creation; and not through the blood of goats and calves, but through His own blood, He entered the holy place once for all, having obtained eternal redemption. For if the blood of goats and bulls and the ashes of a heifer sprinkling those who have been defiled, sanctify for the cleansing of the flesh, how much more will the blood of Christ who through the eternal Spirit offered Himself without blemish to God, cleanse your conscience from dead works to serve the living God?

And for this reason He is the mediator of a new covenant, in order that since a death has taken place for the redemption of the transgressions that were committed under the first covenant (Mosaic), those who have been called may receive the promise of the eternal inheritance. For where a covenant is, there must of necessity be the death of the one who made it. For a covenant is valid only when men are dead, for it is never in force while the one who made it lives.

Therefore even the first covenant was not inaugurated without blood. For when every commandment had been spoken by Moses to all the people according to the Law, he took the blood of the calves and the goats, with water and scarlet wool and hyssop, and sprinkled both the book itself and all the people, saying, "This is the blood of the New Covenant which God commanded you."

And in the same way he sprinkled both the tabernacle and all the vessels of the ministry with the blood, and according to the Law, one may almost say, all things are cleansed with blood, and without shedding of blood there is no forgiveness. Therefore it was necessary for the copies of the things in the heavens to be cleansed with these, but the heavenly things themselves with better sacrifices than these.

For Christ did not enter a holy place made with hands, a mere copy of the true one, but into heaven itself, now to appear in the presence of God for us; nor was it that He should offer Himself often, as the high priest enters the holy place year by year with blood not his own. Otherwise, He would have needed to suffer often since the foundation of the world; but now once at the consummation He has been

manifested to put away sin by the sacrifice of Himself. And inasmuch as it is appointed for men to die once, and after this comes judgment; so Christ also, having been offered once to bear the sin of many, shall appear a second time, not to bear sin, to those who eagerly await Him, for salvation. (Hebrews 9:11-28)

It is important to notice that the passages in Jeremiah thirty-one and Hebrews eight, contrast the New Covenant with the covenant given when Israel came **"out of the land of Egypt."** Again the selection of words is precise. In Deuteronomy twenty-nine, we saw that the children of Israel would be scattered around the world as a result of disobedience to the covenant God made with them when He brought them out of Egypt. Thus the covenant to which they were disobedient was the Mosaic Covenant, not the Abrahamic Covenant. So also, the covenant contrasted in the New Covenant is the Mosaic Covenant, not the Abrahamic Covenant.

In the Bible, the New Covenant *never replaces* the Abrahamic Covenant. Actually, both the Davidic Covenant and the New Covenant are part of the fulfillment of the Abrahamic Covenant. The promise that God would give Israel the land has not yet been fulfilled (we will discuss that later in the last chapter of this book), but the provision in the Abrahamic Covenant that **"all families of the world will be blessed"** was made possible by God sending Jesus, a descendant of King David. In His fulfillment of the Davidic Covenant, and through His death on the cross, Jesus inaugurated and established the New Covenant.

When Jesus and His disciples observed the Passover, shortly before His crucifixion, He instructed them about a new observance that is based on the New Covenant -- an observance celebrated ever since:

And when He had taken some bread and given thanks, He broke it and gave it to them (the disciples) **saying, "This is My body which is given for you; do this in remembrance of Me." And in the same way, He took the cup after they had eaten, saying, "This cup which is poured out for you is the *new covenant* in My blood."** (Luke 22:19-20, italics supplied)

Jesus knew that in the following days He would be crucified at Calvary. But, it is clear from His instructions at that Passover, now referred to as *The Last Supper*, that He knew there was a purpose for His death: He would offer Himself as a redemptive sacrifice for sin and thus put into effect the New Covenant.

Hebrews ten also confirms that the New Covenant is now operative:

He takes away the first in order to establish the second. By this we have been sanctified by the offering of the body of Jesus Christ once and for all.... but He having offered one sacrifice for sins for all time, sat down (because His work on the cross was completed) **at the right hand of God, ... for by one offering He has perfected for all time those who are sanctified. And the Holy Spirit also bears witness to us; for after saying,**

This is the covenant that I will make with them after those days, says the Lord; "I will put My law upon their heart, and upon their mind I will write them."

He then says,

"And their sins and their lawless deeds I will remember no more."

(Both of these quotes are from the New Covenant in Jeremiah.)

... Since therefore, brethren, we have confidence to enter the holy place by the blood of Jesus, by a new and living way which He inaugurated for us ... (Hebrews 10:9-20)

AS NEW TESTAMENT CHRISTIANS, WE ARE PARTICIPATING IN THE FULFILLMENT OF THE COVENANT God MADE WITH ABRAHAM, AND WE ARE LIVING UNDER THE NEW COVENANT PROMISES THAT God GAVE THROUGH JEREMIAH AND EZEKIEL.

In summary, we learn from Christ's words at The Last Supper and the book of Hebrews that the New Covenant promises are now given to those who have trusted in Jesus Christ as their Savior. So, we see that as New Testament

Christians, we are participating in the fulfillment of the promise of blessings God made to Abraham, and we are living under the New Covenant, prophesied by both Jeremiah and Ezekiel.

It is easy to see that to establish the New Covenant, Christ's death was a necessity. Both Jeremiah and Ezekiel mention that a key element of the New Covenant is **"their sins will be forgiven."** Chapter seven of this book traced the *"scarlet cord of redemption"* through the Bible and showed how it led to Jesus, the Lamb of God who made possible forgiveness for sin through His sacrificial offering of Himself on the cross. Hebrews 9:22 explains the reason Christ had to die: **"... for without shedding of blood there is no forgiveness."**

Jeremiah and Ezekiel also talk about a change of the heart. In both passages, God promises to do in us a work of internal reconstruction, which will result in a change of behavior. In Jeremiah, God says, **"I will put My law within them and on their heart I will write it"** (31:33), and in Ezekiel the cause for the change of heart is described as, **"I will put My Spirit within you and cause you to walk according to My statutes"** (36:27). During Jesus' earthly ministry, He spoke of the same thing when He told Nicodemus that a spiritual rebirth was a necessity in order for one to enter into the kingdom of God. Jesus said, **"Truly, truly, I say to you, unless one is born again (of the Spirit), he cannot see the kingdom of God"** (John 3:3).

God promises us internal reconstruction with the result -- a change in our behavior.

We must look at one other passage from the prophets before we move on to the Book of Acts. The prophet Joel spoke about the coming of **"the day of the Lord"** (it was the main topic in Joel's prophecies). Joel described it as a time of judgment and destruction, even a day of darkness and gloom. It is also described as a time when Israel would return to the Lord, that they would never again be a reproach among the nations, and that God would bless them. The day of the Lord was also to be a time when God would **"pour out My Spirit."** The following are a few passages from the Book of Joel:

"Thus you will know that I am in the midst of Israel, and that I am the Lord your God and there is no other; and my people will never be put to shame. And it will come about after this that I will pour out my Spirit on *all mankind*; and your sons and daughters will prophesy, your old men will dream dreams, your young men will see visions. And even on the male and female servants I will pour out my Spirit in those days. ... Then you will know that I am the Lord your God, dwelling in Zion my holy mountain. ... But Judah will be inhabited forever, and Jerusalem for all generations." (Joel 2:27-29, 3:17, 20)

Joel's prophecy that God would **"pour out His Spirit"** is part of his description of the **"day of the Lord"** and the regathering and blessing of Israel. But notice; the promise was for *all mankind.* This is important to consider when examining the Book of Acts.

The Book of Acts is Like a Tapestry Composed of Four Main Strands

The book of Acts is like a beautiful tapestry. There are many threads, and four main strands woven together to form it. It starts with Jesus meeting with his disciples and ascending to heaven. Before he ascended, He promised them He would later return to earth.

1. The Out Pouring of the Holy Spirit

The pouring out of the Holy Spirit and His work in and through the believers in Acts is the first of the four major strands. In Acts, chapter two, we have the initial pouring out of the Holy Spirit, and it is described as a fulfillment of that which the prophet Joel foretold. The activity of the Holy Spirit is so dominant in the book of Acts that it is often referred to as "The Acts of the Holy Spirit," rather than "The Acts of the Apostles." The Holy Spirit continues His work in our lives, even today!

The book of Acts is often referred to as "The Acts of the Holy Spirit," rather than "The Acts of the Apostles."

2. Jesus was Again Offered as Messiah to Israel

Joel's prophecy spoke of **"the day of the Lord,"** an end-times event. This leads to the second strand: A second offer of Jesus as Messiah to Israel. Peter's first two messages (chapters two and three) were both directed to **"Men of Israel."** Notice the words of Peter in his second message (after God had their attention by healing a lame man) in Acts, chapter three:

Men of Israel, why do you marvel at this, or why do you gaze at us, as if by our own power or piety we had made him walk? The God of Abraham, Isaac, and Jacob, the God of our fathers, has glorified His Servant Jesus, the One whom you delivered up and disowned in the presence of Pilate, when he had decided to release Him. But you disowned the Holy and Righteous One, and asked for a murderer to be granted to you, but put to death the Prince of life, the One whom God raised from the dead, a fact to which we are witnesses.

And on the basis of faith in His name, it is the name of Jesus which has strengthened this man whom you see and know; and the faith which comes through Him has given him this perfect health in the presence of you all. And now, brethren, I know that you acted in ignorance, just as your rulers did also. But the things which God announced beforehand by the mouth of all of the prophets, that His Christ should suffer, He has thus fulfilled.

Repent therefore and return, that your sins may be wiped away, in order that times of refreshing may come from the presence of the Lord; and that He may send Jesus, the Christ appointed for you, whom heaven must receive until the period of the restoration of all things about which God spoke by the mouth of His holy prophets from ancient time.

Moses said, "The Lord God shall raise up for you a prophet like Me from your brethren; to Him you shall give heed in

everything He says to you. And it shall be that every soul that does not heed that prophet shall be utterly destroyed from among the people."

"And likewise, all the prophets who have spoken, from Samuel and his successors onward, also announced these days. It is you who are the sons of the prophets, and of the covenant which God made with your fathers, saying to Abraham, 'And in your seed all the families of the earth shall be blessed.' For you first, God raised up His Servant, and sent Him to bless you by turning every one of you from your wicked ways." (Acts 3:12-26)

When one analyzes Peter's message, it is clear that his emphasis is on the fulfillment of the promises God gave to Israel in the Abrahamic Covenant. Peter clearly referred to the promises of the *seed* and *blessings* when he spoke to the assembled Israelites of **"the restoration of all things about which God spoke by the mouth of His holy prophets"** (Acts 13:21). The word he translated *restoration* is a word that means to restore to the rightful owner, a reference that would include, in the minds of the Israelites, the promise of the *land.*

In the previous chapter, we saw that in Jesus' parable in Matthew, twenty-two, Jesus said servants would be sent a second time to those who were invited. In this message, Peter again offers Jesus as Messiah to Israel, and states that if they would repent and return to the Lord, their sins would be forgiven and God would **"send Jesus the Christ"** (the Messiah).

We do not know what would have happened if the nation of Israel had accepted Jesus as the Messiah when He was first offered to them in the Gospel accounts, or what would have happened if the Israelites had accepted Him as Messiah when He was offered to them a second time during the time of the book of Acts.

Again we refer to the Book of Job where we learn that *no purpose of God can be thwarted* (Job 42:2 and 42:8). The death of Jesus was a necessity. It is probable that if the Jews had rallied behind Jesus, the *Romans* would have crucified Him.

The charge that the Jews were the killers of Jesus is meaningless, for both Isaiah 53:10 and Acts 2:23 tell us that the offering of Jesus, the Messiah, as a sacrifice for our sin was part of God's plan. That His crucifixion was carried out by Israel, His chosen people whom He loves, serves as a picture of His "*in spite of*" love for all of us. **"But God demonstrates His own love toward us, in that while we were yet sinners, Christ died for us"** (Romans 5:8).

Both offers of Jesus as Messiah were legitimate, even though God knew, in His foreknowledge, that they would be rejected. We must also recognize that God's sovereign plan included the establishment of the Church. But, apart from the potential for the end-time events, described by Joel, happening at that time, it is hard to see why Peter would have referred to the events in Acts two as a fulfillment of the prophecy of Joel. If **the Day of the Lord** could have potentially come at that time, then Peter's reference to Joel makes perfect sense.

The book of Acts records that Jesus was offered and rejected a second time by the Israelites. The offer included not only Jesus as Messiah to the nation, but the good news of forgiveness for sin and the power of the Holy Spirit (both New Covenant promises).

Peter first preached this **"Good News"** in Jerusalem, and likewise, the Apostle Paul always went **"to the Jew first"** (Romans 1:16) in his journeys. This second offering of Jesus as Messiah to Israel is a major strand that weaves all the way through the Book of Acts. As the second rejection was taking place, we also see the beginning of the **"gathering together all they found, both bad and good, and the wedding hall was filled with dinner guests,"** foretold in the parable Jesus gave in Matthew twenty-two.

The Messianic promises were never exclusively for Israel. Yes, Israel was the nation God elected to use as His *channel* to minister to the whole world. But, starting with Abraham, and repeatedly thereafter, the Bible tells us God was going to bless Israel so that **"all nations of the earth would be blessed."** By application, the principal also applies to us today. God wants to bless us so that we can be a blessing to others.

3. The Establishment of the Church

This brings up the third major strand in the book of Acts. In Matthew sixteen, Jesus, using the future tense, said; **"I will build My Church."** The word *ekklesia*, translated *church*, was a commonly used word in both the Greek and Roman empires. It literally meant "the called out ones." It was first used by the Greeks to refer to a "legally called out assembly" for a political gathering of a city-state.

If Greek were the language of the United States, the delegates at the Republican and Democrat political conventions could be referred to as a church. Some might say that is a bit of a stretch, but in Acts nineteen the word is twice translated *assembly*: in verse twenty-two when speaking of an *angry mob*, and in verse thirty-nine when speaking of a *lawful assembly*. In both contexts, and in other secular usages in that day, the word was used of a group of people that were united behind a common purpose or goal.

THe CHuRch is noT A buildiNq. IT is A body of believers wHo ARe iNdwelT by tHe Holy SpiRiT.

In Matthew sixteen, Jesus added a modifier and called His assembly **"My Church."** His words could be paraphrased, **"My Called Out Ones,"** or even **"My Delegates."** Ephesians two teaches more of His Church's character. In His Church, Jesus is the Head, the members (true believers in Christ) are the Body, it is a dwelling place for the Holy Spirit, and is composed of both Jews and Gentiles. In the New Testament, the Church is not a building. It is the *people*. We sometimes refer to a church building as "God's house," but the truth is that God does not now reside in buildings. Today, He only enters a building, in a special way, if a believer enters it -- <u>We *are His sanctuary.*</u>

THe qRowTH of tHe Body of CHRisT coNTiNues oN todAy.

Sometimes the word *church* is used to describe all believers (the Universal Church) and sometimes it is used to describe a local assembly of believers (a local Church). The Book of Acts tells us how the Church was born and about some of its early struggles and victories -- yes it had both. The growth of the Church, the Body of Jesus Christ, did not end in the Book of Acts, it is still growing today as others trust in Jesus as their Savior and become part of His body.

4. The Message of the Apostles About Jesus

The fourth major strand used to weave the tapestry of the Book of Acts is the message of the Apostles about Jesus. Five main points are proclaimed about Him, over and over again:

1. He was the Messiah promised in the Old Testament.
2. His death was redemptive.
3. He rose from the grave.
4. He presently lives through believers by the indwelling of the Holy Spirit.
5. He is going to return to the earth in the future.

The Book of Acts started in Jerusalem; the message was then carried to Judea and Samaria, and on to the uttermost parts of the world. Acts records the history of Israel's rejection, the establishment of the Church, and the events that occurred during the writing of the New Testament epistles. The final chapter of the Acts of the Holy Spirit has not yet been written. Even today, believers are a part of the movement of God's Spirit that began in the Book of Acts.

The message of the Church is still the same as that proclaimed in the Book of Acts:

1. Jesus is the Messiah promised in the Old Testament!
2. Jesus died on the cross as the sacrificial Lamb of God to redeem us from our sinful rebellion against God!
3. Jesus rose victoriously from the grave on Easter Sunday morning. Because He lives, we can have eternal life!

4. Jesus is alive today. He sent us the Holy Spirit who wants to live His life through us. We (the Church) are His body.

5. Jesus is coming again! When He comes, He will bring judgment for those who have rejected Him, and the blessed hope for those who have placed their faith in Him.

Read carefully the words of the Apostle John in I John 5:11-13:

> **And the witness is this, that God has given us eternal life, and this life is in his Son. He who has the Son has the life; he who does not have the Son of God does not have the life. These things I have written to you who believe in the name of the Son of God, in order that you may know that you have eternal life.**

If you have not yet placed your faith in Jesus Christ as your Savior, you need to do so before we move on to the Epistles -- God's love letters to those who have trusted in Jesus as their Savior. If He is not yet your Savior, reading the Epistles would be like reading someone else's very personal mail. If you have not trusted in Jesus, go back and read Chapter Six again. Then make the prayer at the end of that chapter -- your prayer. Jesus will forgive your sin, come and dwell in you, and give you eternal life. Then these love letters will be for you, too!

SUMMARY of CHAPTER NINE:

In Jeremiah, God promised to give a New Covenant to Israel. Concepts from the New Covenant were repeated in the prophecies of Ezekiel and Joel. Both foretold that God was going to send the Holy Spirit to indwell men.

Joel's prophecy pointed to an end-time event called, **"The Day of the Lord."** After Jesus ascended into heaven, on the day of Pentecost, God poured out His Spirit on the believers in Jerusalem.

Four major strands are seen in the tapestry woven together by Luke, the author of *The Acts of the Apostles:*

The first strand was the pouring out of the Holy Spirit. The activities of the Holy Spirit so dominate the Book of Acts that it is often called "The Acts of the Holy Spirit."

The second strand was the reoffering of Jesus as Messiah to the nation of Israel. In Peter's sermons, he proclaimed Jesus as Messiah and Paul always went to the Jew first.

The third strand in Acts is the fulfilling of the promise Jesus made in Matthew sixteen, when He said, **"I will build My Church."** The Greek word translated *church* means "the called out ones." Jesus added the modifier "My," and His Church is composed of those whom the Lord has called to Himself, both Jews and Gentiles.

The fourth strand in Acts is the message they proclaimed about Jesus. They boldly told everyone: Jesus is the Messiah promised in the Old Testament; He died on the cross as the sacrificial Lamb of God to redeem us from our sin; and He rose from the grave on Easter Sunday morning. They asserted that because He lives, we can have eternal life, that He is alive today, and He wants to live His life through us.

Chapter 10
Know ... Reckon ... Yield

With Israel having rejected Jesus as Messiah, God is now using the Church to accomplish His purpose to fulfill the promise He made to Abraham that **"all families of the world will be blessed."** In the last chapter of this book we will look again at the prophecies about **"the day of the Lord"** and how they will ultimately be fulfilled for the nation of Israel and the world. But, before we do, it is vital that we examine the New Covenant principles we live by today.

We have seen that Hebrews chapter eight quotes the New Covenant from Jeremiah, and that Hebrews chapter nine explains that the New Covenant was inaugurated by Jesus' death on the cross. This leads to the declaration in Hebrews ten that the New Covenant was established to replace the Law. It reads **"He takes away the first** (the Law) **in order to establish the second** (the New Covenant). **By this will, we have been sanctified** (made holy) **through the offering of the body of Jesus Christ once for all... For by one offering He has perfected for all time those who are sanctified** (are being made holy)." The next few verses explain that as a result of this sacrifice, we can draw near to God, holding fast our faith, because **"He who promised is faithful"** (Hebrews 10:9-23).

In chapter four of this book, we learned that true biblical faith is our trusting response to God's promises. Hebrews, chapters eight through ten, tell us that those who have placed their faith in Jesus partake of the promises God gave to Israel in the New Covenant. Yes, God's promises were originally given to

Israel, and in the future there will be an ultimate fulfillment for Israel, but the *good news* is that New Covenant promises belong to us today. In God's love letters to us (the epistles), we are told we can walk by faith in these promises!

In the King James Version, the word translated *testament* in Hebrews nine is translated *covenant* in Hebrews, chapter eight. While the title *New Testament* is used to describe the twenty-seven books of the Bible from Matthew through Revelation, the title is a synonym for the *New Covenant.* Today, those who have received Jesus Christ as Savior are members of His body, the Church, and are living under the New Covenant. Consequently, we are to **"draw near** (to God) **with a sincere heart in full assurance of faith, ... for He who promised is faithful"** (Hebrews 10:22-23). (Again, notice that true faith rests on our believing that God is faithful in fulfilling His promises.)

As believers, living under the New Covenant, it is particularly important that we notice the cause and effect relationships expressed in both Jeremiah and Ezekiel. Before accepting Christ, I assumed that living a good life was the *cause* that would produce the desired *effect* (a right relationship with God). In these passages we discover that the *cause* is a work of God in one's life with the *effect* being the life that is led. This is particularly clear in Ezekiel thirty-six where it says; **"I will put my Spirit within you and *cause* you to walk in My statutes."** The *cause* is **"My Spirit within you."** (Ezekiel 36:27 NASB). The *effect* is to **"walk in My statutes."** The same idea is present in Jeremiah 31:33 (NASB) where it says; **"I will put My law within them, and on their heart I will write it; and I will be their God and they shall be My people"**

The cause is "My Spirit within you."
The effect is to "walk in My statutes."

"My law within them" refers to the principles taught in God's law. They have not changed. For those who were under it, the law was external. For those who are indwelt by the

Spirit, it is internal. Expressed another way, we don't follow an external set of do's and don'ts. We now have an internal desire to live for God in a way that will not violate His law, because we are indwelt by His Holy Spirit.

These principles are discussed in the Epistles, the letters written by the Apostles (during the time span of the book of Acts) to people living under the New Covenant. There are far too many subjects covered in the Epistles to attempt to cover them all in this book, but we will examine one overriding principle in this chapter and two promises from the New Covenant in the following two chapters.

We appropriate the New Covenant promises by faith

The overriding principle is that we live under the New Covenant by *faith*. It's not an accident that the great faith chapter, Hebrews eleven, follows Hebrews chapter ten. God established the Abrahamic Covenant with Abraham because he was a man of *faith*. As ones who live under the New Covenant (part of the fulfillment of the Abrahamic covenant), we are to live by *faith*. The life of Abraham demonstrated that faith is not a subjective thing. In Chapter four of this book, the life of Abraham helped us discover five factors of a fixed faith. Again, the five factors are:

1. Abraham believed that God is the living God.
2. Abraham believed God has made promises.
3. Abraham believed God has the power to fulfill His promises.
4. Abraham believed God will be faithful in fulfilling His promises.
5. Abraham's faith had "legs that walk."

In the sixth chapter of his great doctrinal letter to the Romans, the Apostle Paul gives us instructions on how to give our faith "legs that walk." In this chapter, we learn the first three steps in a walk of faith:

What shall we say then? Are we to continue in sin that grace might increase? May it never be! How shall we who died to sin live in it? Or do you not know that all of us who have been baptized into Christ Jesus have been baptized into His death. We have been buried with Him through baptism into death, in order that as Christ was raised from the dead through the glory of the Father, so we too might walk in newness of life.

For if we have become united with Him in the likeness of His death, certainly we shall be also in the likeness of His resurrection, knowing this, that our old self was crucified with Him, that our body of sin might be done away with, that we should no longer be slaves to sin; for he who has died is freed from sin.

Now if we have died with Christ, we believe that we shall also live with Him, knowing that Christ, having been raised from the dead, is never to die again; death no longer is master over Him. For the death that He died, He died to sin, once for all; but the life that He lives, He lives to God.

Even so consider yourselves to be dead to sin, but alive to God in Christ Jesus. There-fore do not let sin reign in your mortal body that you should obey its lusts, and do not go on presenting the members of your body as instruments of unrighteousness; but to present ourselves to God as those alive from the dead, and your members as instruments of righteousness to God. (Romans 6:3-14)

We must KNOW what we are and have in Christ

The first step in faith is for us to *know* who we are and what we have in Christ (i.e., what He has promised us). In Romans 6:3-10 we learn that as believers we have entered into a union with Jesus Christ. When He died on the cross, we died with Him; when He arose -- we rose with Him. We are to see ourselves as totally identified with Jesus, and *know* He now wants to live His life through us. So the first step is *knowing*. *Knowing* what we are, and have, in Christ.

There are many passages in the New Testament that teach about things we can *know* we have in Christ. We should apply this step of faith from Romans six as we walk with God -- a walk in faith, based on knowledge of His promises.

We must believe it with our whole being

Romans 6:11 explains the second step in our walk: We are to **consider** that which we know to be true. The King James translation uses the word *reckon* instead of *consider.* In the original Greek, it is a word from the world of accounting that meant to write it down in one's official records. It is claiming that what God says about us is a veritable truth. You only write something in your official records if you know, for sure, that it is true. To reckon something is to believe it with your whole being.

WE ARE TO SEE OURSELVES AS TOTALLY IDENTIFIED WITH JESUS, AND KNOW HE WANTS TO LIVE HIS LIFE THROUGH US AND yield THE RIGHT OF WAY IN OUR LIVES TO HIM.

Romans 6:13 commends the third step: We are to *present* ourselves to God to be used as His instruments. The King James Version translates that word *yield.* You could say we are to *yield the right of way in our lives to God.* We need to give Him first place, and allow Him to direct our steps. Our rebellious sin nature protests: "Do your own thing!" But, when we do, our old sin nature *dominates.* So, yield the control of your life to God. As an infinitely wise and loving Father, you can trust Him to give you peace, purpose, and spiritual fulfillment.

God PROMISES VICTORY OVER SIN TO THOSE who yield THE RIGHT OF WAY IN THEIR LIVES TO HIM

This walk of faith has a natural consequence: **"For sin shall not be master over you, for you are not under law, but under grace"** (Romans 6:14). God promises victory over sin to those who yield the right of way in their lives to Him. We stake our claim to this promise by *knowing* who we are and what we have in Christ, *considering it to be true,* and *yielding* the right of way in our lives to God. The result:

"Sin -- It ain't gonna reign no more!"

Summary of Chapter Ten:

From the New Covenant we learned that the cause in our life is the work of the Lord (**I will put My Spirit within them**), with the effect being the life that is led (**and cause them to walk according to My statutes**). To appropriate these New Covenant promises we need faith that **knows** God's promises to us, **reckons** them to be true, and then **yields** the right of way in our lives to Him.

Chapter 11
Never Forget You're Forgiven

The New Covenant includes two very important, related promises. In this chapter, we will look at the first of these promises. It will provide us with a foundation for the second promise, which we will examine in the following chapter. The first is the cornerstone of the *Gospel*, which means *Good News*. The *Good News* is that Jesus, the Messiah, came and died on the cross to pay in full the price for our sin, and thus to give us *total and complete forgiveness*. But, in spite of having this promise, there are many Christians who still live with a burden of guilt. They are like wealthy men who are unaware of their riches and are therefore living in poverty. Read the Apostle Peter's comments in II Peter 1:2-11:

Grace and peace be multiplied to you in the knowledge of God and of Jesus our Lord; seeing that His divine power has granted to us everything pertaining to life and godliness, through the true knowledge of Him who called us by His own glory and excellence. For by these He has granted to us His precious and magnificent promises, in order that by them you might become partakers of the divine nature, having escaped the corruption that is in the world by lust.

Now this very reason also, applying all diligence, in your faith supply moral excellence, and in your moral excellence, knowledge; and in your knowledge, self-control; and in your self-control, perseverance; and in your perseverance, godliness; and in your godliness, brotherly kindness; and in your brotherly kindness, love. For if these qualities are yours and

are increasing, they render you neither useless nor unfruitful in the true knowledge of our Lord Jesus Christ. For he who lacks these qualities is blind or short sighted having forgotten his purification from his former sins. Therefore, brethren, be all the more diligent to make certain about His calling and choosing you; for as long as you practice these things you will never stumble; for in this way the entrance into the eternal kingdom of our Lord and Savior Jesus Christ will be abundantly supplied to you.

This passage teaches that **"His divine power has granted to us everything pertaining to life and godliness ... by ... His ... precious promises."** This being true, we should therefore be experiencing a quality of life that exhibits the moral excellence and other characteristics Peter described. But, Peter sees a problem. There are many who have received Christ, but who do not have these qualities in their lives. Peter knows why they are living in spiritual poverty, and he gives the reason in verse nine: **"... he who lacks these qualities,** (the qualities of life Peter has described) **is blind or short sighted, having forgotten his purification from his former sins."**

If forgetting you are forgiven will keep you from having a victorious life, then knowing you are forgiven will produce victory in your life.

Peter tells us, if someone is not experiencing the victorious Christian life, it is because **"they have forgotten they are forgiven!"** Now, think about this: If forgetting you are forgiven will keep you from having these victorious qualities, then what will produce them? The answer is obvious: *"Knowing I am forgiven!"* When a believer walks under a burden of guilt, he is saying, "I do not believe you, God, when you tell me that Jesus paid <u>in full</u> the price for my sin!" It is unbelief, pure and simple -- a denial of one of God's precious promises!

In my younger years, I played in a lot of golf tournaments. If someone asks me "What is the most important thing one must do to win a golf tournament?" I reply, "Forget the shots you miss!" I learned, by experience, that if I thought about the shots I missed, it would cause me to make more bad shots. When I put my awful shots out of my mind, I could relax and swing correctly. The same principle is true in the game of life.

After repenting of our sin, God wants us to put it behind us. In Philippians 3:13-14 the Apostle Paul wrote, **"... but one thing I do: forgetting what lies behind and reaching forward to what lies ahead, I press on toward the goal for the prize of the upward call of God in Christ Jesus."**

Dwelling on your past sin is like an anchor that will pull you under and drown you in more sin and guilt

---

Dwelling on our past sins will not give us victory over future temptations to sin. Thinking about our past sin only serves as an anchor that will pull us under, and we will drown in additional sins. To have victory, we need to put our sin behind us. "But," you ask, "how?"

To have victory, you must put your sin behind you!

The apostle John tells us how to deal with our sin:

And this is the message we have heard from Him and announce to you, that God is light, and in Him there is no darkness at all. If we say that we have fellowship with Him and yet walk in the darkness, we lie and do not practice the truth; but if we walk in the light as He Himself is in the light, we have fellowship with one another, and the blood of Jesus His Son cleanses us from all sin.

If we say that we have no sin, we are deceiving ourselves, and the truth is not in us. If we confess our sins, He is faithful and righteous to forgive us our sins and to cleanse us

from all unrighteousness. If we say that we have not sinned, we make Him a liar, and His word is not in us. My little children, I am writing these things to you that you may not sin. (I John 1:5-2:2)

The first question one must ask is, "What does it mean to walk in the light?" It is obvious this passage is not describing a life without any sin, for it says: **"If we walk in the light... the blood of Jesus His Son** (continually) **cleanses us from all sin."**

The key is to understand the difference between darkness and light -- that darkness conceals, but light reveals. If we are walking in darkness, we try to hide and conceal any sin in our lives *from* God. If we are walking in the light, and we trip and fall, we put the sin out in God's holy light and *reveal it to* Him.

Darkness conceals, but light reveals

To deny the reality of our sin is tragic. In the above passage, John calls it *a lie that deceives ourselves* (it is a rarity that it ever deceives anyone else). We should add; it is a *lethal lie.* Outwardly, we may profess our innocence, but down inside, we know that such denial is pure hypocrisy. Some people try to overcome their feelings of guilt by lowering their standards of right and wrong. But that is merely another form of denial, and it does not bring peace to the heart -- depression and other neurotic disorders, yes. But never peace.

Walking in darkness = hiding our sin from God

I John 1:9 gives us God's solution for our sin problem: **"If we confess our sins, He is faithful and righteous to forgive us our sins and to cleanse us from all unrighteousness."** A literal translation of the Greek word for *confess* is "to say the same thing as another." When we confess our sin, we say to God the same thing about our sin that He says. First, we agree that it is sin! But, we also agree that, when Jesus died on the cross, He paid in full the price for our sin! Therefore we *know* God we are forgiven.

Walking in the light = confessing our sin to God

In the New Covenant, Jeremiah records an additional truth. God not only forgives our sin, but **"their sin I will remember no more."** If when we confess our sin to God, He both forgives and forgets it, why should we brood over it? There is no good reason. We need to claim His forgiveness and put the sin behind us. This should not be taken as a license for more sin. Rather, when we experience His love, we are motivated by a burning desire to walk closer to Him.

In I John 2:1, John says the reason he is writing these things is **"that you may not sin."** So the path to victory over sin is to **"walk in the light,"** not hiding our sin from God, rather, instantly, whenever we are aware of sin in our lives, confessing it to God, and agreeing with God that **"Jesus paid in full the price for _my_ sin"** (John 19:30 paraphrase -- it needs to be personal). Then we put the sin behind us. Since God forgets it, we should too. While we should repent and feel remorse for our sin, when it happens, continual brooding over our sin is unbelief. It amounts to a denial that Jesus paid *in full* the price for our sin!

Jesus is Our Advocate in Heaven

The remainder of I John 2:1-2 paints a beautiful picture: **And if anyone sins, we have an advocate with the Father, Jesus Christ the righteous; and He Himself is the propitiation for our sins; and not for ours only, but also for those of the whole world.**

These verses picture what happens in heaven when a believer sins. The "accuser of the brethren" (Satan) points and says, "God, look at that sin!" But we have an *advocate*. The *Berkeley Translation* renders the word *advocate*, **"a council of defense."** Picture yourself as a defendant in a court room. The prosecution points to your transgressions. But you have Jesus as your attorney defending you, and He makes an astounding defense. He proclaims, **"When I died on the cross, I paid the penalty for that sin. I satisfied the demand of holiness to punish that sin."**

That's the heart and core of the Good News we find in the Bible. *Jesus took our place, as our substitute, and paid in full the price for our sins.* We are to live by faith. We give our faith legs by **"walking in the light,"** confessing our sin to God, and agreeing with God that He has forgiven and forgotten our sin.

Since We are Forgiven, We Need to Forgive Others!

Before leaving I John, we must look at the other side of the coin of forgiveness. John brings it up in I John, chapter two: **The one who says he is in the light and yet hates his brother is in the darkness until now. The one who loves his brother abides in the light and there is no cause for stumbling in him. But the one who hates his brother is in the darkness and walks in the darkness, and does not know where he is going because the darkness has blinded his eyes.** (I John 2:9-11)

The Apostle Paul expressed the same idea:

Let all bitterness and wrath and anger and clamor and slander be put away from you along with all malice, and be kind to one another, tender-hearted, forgiving each other, just as God in Christ also has forgiven you. (Ephesians 4:31-32)

Oh, how many there are who want to *experience* God's forgiveness in their own lives, but find themselves living under a burden of guilt because they are *unwilling* to give up their bitterness toward others. The subject here is not actual forgiveness. If someone has truly accepted Jesus as Savior, there are many passages that teach he is forgiven by God. But, it is possible to be forgiven by God, yet to walk in blind darkness, unable to see or experience being forgiven. It is impossible to walk in the light and hold bitterness in our hearts toward others -- for any reason.

Jesus expressed this when He suggested how we should pray. He said, **"And forgive us our debts, as we forgive our debtors"** (Matthew 6:12). It is a tragic fact that many Christians repeat the Lord's Prayer every Sunday morning -- then walk out of church with bitterness in their hearts toward others. Sometimes the bitterness is toward someone who was sitting in the next pew!

It is impossible to walk in the light and hold bitterness in your heart toward others -- for any reason

---

Bitterness may in some cases cause some remorse in the other person, but there are nothing but negative consequences for the person who is bitter. For the bitter person, the unforgiving spirit is devastating. Again, hear John's warning, **"But the one who hates his brother is in the darkness and walks in the darkness, and does not know where he is going because the darkness has blinded his eyes."** (I John 2:11)

We find an example in the Old Testament book of Job, how we should *NOT* walk: **"But the anger of Elihu ... burned; against Job, his anger burned because he justified himself before God"** (Job 32:2 NASB). This verse, from the oldest book in the Bible, speaks volumes. Self-righteousness inevitably produces a judgmental attitude in one's heart. The self-righteous person looks with contempt at other's sinful actions, but then turns around and makes excuses to justify his own sinful behavior.

The Apostle Paul tells us of the attitude we should have toward the sins of others. It is vital that we observe that Paul includes a warning in his instructions: **Brothers, if someone is caught in a sin, you who are spiritual should restore him gently. But watch yourself, or you also may be tempted** (Galatians 6:1 NIV). Never, ever look at the sin of another person and say to yourself, "I would not do something like that!"

That attitude is a deadly trap! The wise man knows; "There, but for the grace of God, go I."

In these passages, we see that forgiving others is related to seeing ourselves as guilty and forgiven. In fact, the secret to being able to forgive someone else is to first see ourselves as guilty and forgiven. One of Jesus' most powerful parables was on this subject:

Then Peter came and said to Him, "Lord, how often shall my brother sin against me and I forgive him? Up to seven times?" Jesus said to him, "I do not say to you, up to seven times, but up to seventy times seven. For this reason the kingdom of heaven may be compared to a certain king who wished to settle accounts with his slaves. And when he had begun to settle them, there was brought to him one who owed him ten thousand talents (several million dollars). **But since he did not have the means to repay, his lord commanded him to be sold, along with his wife and children and all that he had, and repayment to be made. The slave therefore falling down, prostrated himself before him, saying, 'Have patience with me, and I will repay you everything.' And the lord of that slave felt compassion and released him and forgave him the debt.**

But that slave went out and found one of his fellow slaves who owed him a hundred denarii (about a day's wages); **and he seized him and began to choke him, saying, 'Pay back what you owe.' So his fellow-slave fell down and began to entreat him saying, 'Have patience with me and I will repay you.' He was unwilling however, but went and threw him in prison until he should pay back what was owed.**

So when his fellow-slaves saw what had happened, they were deeply grieved and came and reported to their lord all that had happened. Then summoning him, his lord said to him, 'You wicked slave, I forgave you all that debt because you entreated me. Should you not also have had mercy on your fellow slave, even as I had mercy on you?' And his lord, moved with anger, handed him over to the torturers until he should repay all that was owed him. So shall My heavenly Father also do to you, if each of you does not forgive his brother from your heart." (Matthew 18:21-35)

In this parable the unjust steward's debt to the king was a gigantic amount. In the comparison, the debt of the fellow slave was but a pittance. This is a picture of our sin against God, and the sin of others against us. The sin of others against us is always a pittance when compared to our sin against God. God forgives us and commands us to forgive others.

It's not uncommon for God to hear from one of His children, "I can't forgive them! God, if you expect me to forgive them, You must not understand what they did to me!" In Matthew eighteen, Jesus gave us God's response. We could paraphrase it: **"Your problem is that you are not seeing your sin against Me as it actually is, greater than the other person's sin against you! I forgave you, and you need to forgive them!"** Oh, how we need to comprehend this truth!

THE SIN OF OTHERS AGAINST US IS ALWAYS A PITTANCE
WHEN COMPARED TO OUR SIN AGAINST God.

It is important to remember that God never asks us to do something that He will not help us do. As one who has invited Jesus Christ to live His life through you, *you can forgive that other person.* First acknowledge to God that your sin against God is greater than anyone else's sin against you, and that God has forgiven you. Then, *knowing* your body is a temple of the Holy Spirit, ask God to give you His forgiving attitude toward the other person. Since He *lives* in you, when you yield to Him, He will give you His forgiving spirit toward others.

Most of the psychologists and counselors in the world would have to find other occupations if we would only learn, and apply, the lesson from Jesus' parable about the unjust steward! It is imperative that we forgive one another. Why? Because God, in Christ, has forgiven us! *No excuses for bitterness are ever accepted -- No, not one!*

And forgive us our debts, as we forgive our debtors.

The Lord's Prayer - Matthew 6:12

Summary of Chapter Eleven:

One of the promises in the New Covenant is that we will be forgiven for our sin. The apostle Peter tells us that many believers walk in defeat because they have forgotten they are forgiven. This tells us that a key to having victory over sin is to remember we are forgiven.

We remember we are forgiven by "walking in the light," not hiding our sin from God, but confessing it to Him and claiming our forgiveness, because Jesus died for our sins..

Claiming *our* forgiveness is but one side of the coin. Just as God has forgiven us, *we* must forgive others. The parable of the unjust steward reminds us that *our* sin against God is far greater than anyone else's sin against us. God has forgiven us the *major* debt, therefore we must forgive others for their minor debt. The keys to be able to forgive others are first, to see ourselves as being guilty, but forgiven, and second to ask God to forgive through us by the power of the Holy Spirit.

Chapter 12
More Than A Heart Transplant

In the New Covenant, God gave another very significant promise. He promised that He will reconstruct us from the inside out -- that He will perform in us a spiritual heart transplant. In the Book of Ezekiel, God said He would **"put My Spirit within you and cause you to walk according to My statutes."** In the Book of Joel God said, **"I will pour out My Spirit on all people."** The broad context of the Bible would preclude this from applying to every person in the world, but there is no doubt it is a promise that includes *people* from every nation in the world.

In modern medicine, a heart transplant has become a somewhat common operation. In such an operation, the surgeon replaces the old defective heart with one that functions well -- but the new heart is not able to do anything other than what the patient's previously healthy heart had done. The heart transplant God promises in the New Covenant is much better -- better than the heart we had when we were born! When God gives us a new heart, He renews us spiritually. It is far more wonderful than a physical heart transplant!

WHEN God gives us a new heart, it is better than the heart we had when we were born.

On the day of Pentecost (Acts chapter two), God poured out the Holy Spirit, in a supernatural way, on the disciples who were Jerusalem. This amazing event created quite a commotion:

Then Peter stepped forward with the eleven other apostles, and shouted to the crowd ... "In the last days, God said, 'I

will pour out My Spirit upon all mankind. Your sons and daughters will prophesy, and your young men will see visions, and your old men will dream dreams. In those days I will pour out My Spirit upon all My servants, men and women alike, and they will prophesy. And I will cause wonders in the heavens above and signs on the earth below ... And anyone who calls on the name of the Lord will be saved.'

People of Israel, listen! God publicly endorsed Jesus of Nazareth by doing wonderful miracles, wonders, and signs through Him, as you well know. But you followed God's pre-arranged plan. With the help of lawless Gentiles, you nailed Him to the cross and murder Him. However, God released Him from the horrors of death and raised Him back to life again, for death could not keep Him in its grip. King David said this about Him:

'I know the Lord is always with me. I will not be shaken for He is right beside me. No wonder my heart is filled with joy, and my mouth shouts His praises! My body rests in hope. For you will not leave my soul among the dead, or allow your Holy One to rot in the grave. You have shown me the way of life, and You will give me wonderful joy in Your presence.'

Dear brothers, think about this! David wasn't referring to himself when he spoke these words I have quoted, for he died and was buried, and his tomb is still here among us. But he was a prophet, and he knew God had promised with an oath that one of David's own descendants would sit on David's throne as the Messiah. David was looking into the future and predicting the Messiah's resurrection. He was saying that the Messiah would not be left among the dead and that His body would not rot in the grave.

This prophecy was speaking of Jesus, whom God raised from the dead, and we are all witnesses of this. And now He sits on the throne of highest honor in heaven, at God's right hand. And the Father, as He promised, gave Him the Holy Spirit to pour out upon us, just as you see and hear today. For David himself never ascended into heaven, yet he said, 'The Lord said to my Lord, Sit in honor at my right hand until I humble your enemies, making them a footstool under your feet.'

So let it be clearly known by everyone in Israel that God has made this Jesus whom you crucified to be both Lord and Messiah!"

Peter's words convicted them deeply, and they said to him and to the other apostles, "Brothers, what should we do?"

Peter replied, "Each of you must turn from sins and turn to God, and be baptized in the name of Jesus Christ for the forgiveness of your sins. Then you also will receive the gift of the Holy Spirit. This promise is to you and to your children, and even to the Gentiles -- all you who have been called by the Lord our God." (Acts 2:14-39 NLT)

Peter tells us, **"... the promise of Holy Spirit"**... is **"as many as the Lord our God shall call to Himself"** (Acts 2:33 & 39 NASB). The Greek word translated *as many* is translated the same way in the Gospel of John when it says, **"As many as received Him, to them He gave the right to become children of God, even to those who believe in His name"** (John 1:12). It means ALL (including Gentiles).

Paul, speaking against a gross sin practiced by some believers in Corinth, (apparently they were visiting prostitutes - I Corinthians 6:15-18) exhorted them, **"Do you not know that your body is a temple of the Holy Spirit, who is in you ..."** (I Corinthians 6:19). Notice, we again come upon that word *know*. If we are to give legs to our faith we must *know* who we are and what we have in Christ. Apparently what these men did not know, or had forgotten, was that as believers they were indwelt by the Holy Spirit.

The authors of the Epistles wrote with the assumption that the Holy Spirit dwells within the readers. Paul wrote, **"But if the Spirit of Him who raised Jesus from the dead dwells in you, He who raised Christ Jesus from the dead will also give life to your mortal bodies through His Spirit who indwells you"** (Romans 8:11). In Ephesians, Paul wrote, **"In Him, you also, after listening to the message of trust, the gospel of your salvation -- having also believed, you were sealed in Him with the Holy Spirit of promise, who is given as a pledge of our inheritance, with a view to the redemption of God's own possession, to the praise of His glory."** (Ephesians 1:13-14)

The Epistles were written with the assumption
that the Holy Spirit dwelt within the readers.

In Ephesians one, Paul also prays that the readers will have their eyes opened to the fact that the power within them is the *same* power that raised Christ from the grave: "**I pray that the eyes of your heart may be enlightened, so you may know what is the hope of His calling, what are the riches of the glory of His inheritance in the saints, and what is the surpassing greatness of His power toward us who believe. These are in accordance with the working of the strength of His might which He brought about in Christ when He raised Him from the dead, and seated Him at His right hand in heavenly places**" (Ephesians 1:18-20). The word translated as *power* is the root for our English word, *dynamite*. Summarizing these verses: Paul wants us to have the eyes of our hearts opened that we may *know* that we have the Holy Spirit, who raised Christ from the dead, dwelling within us, and that the Holy Spirit provides us with dynamite power for living.

We need to know that the power of the Holy Spirit within
us is the same power that raised Christ from the grave.

As mentioned above, Paul wrote to some believers, who were apparently involved in gross sin, that their bodies were the temple of the Holy Spirit. From this passage we learn that though we are indwelt by the Holy Spirit, this by itself does not assure us of living victoriously. I Thessalonians 5:19 exhorts us "**Do not quench the Spirit**" and Ephesians 4:30 exhorts us "**... do not grieve the Holy Spirit of God ....**" When a believer sins it both quenches and grieves the Holy Spirit. But, Paul does not tell them that as a result of sinful actions the Holy Spirit departs. No, Paul told those men, "**Or do you not know, your body is a temple of the Holy Spirit, who is in you, whom you have from God, and that you are not your own. For you have been bought with** a price; therefore glorify God in your body" (I Corinthians 6:19-20). Since our bodies are the temples of the Holy Spirit, we are to allow Him to live through us a life that will glorify God. We do this by walking, yielded to the Holy Spirit who indwells us, thus unleashing the power of the Holy Spirit, so that He can produce victory in our lives. Galatians 5:16-25 emphasizes this important truth:

But I say, walk by the Spirit, and you will not carry out the desire of the flesh. For the flesh sets its desire against the Spirit, and the Spirit against the flesh; for these are in opposition to one another; so that you may not do the things that you please. But if you are led by the Spirit, you are not under the Law.

Now the deeds of the flesh are evident, which are: immorality, impurity, sensuality, idolatry, sorcery, enmities, strife, jealousy, outbursts of anger, disputes, dissensions, factions, envyings, drunkenness, carousings, and things like these, of which I forewarn you just as I have forewarned you that those who practice such things shall not inherit the kingdom of God. But the fruit of the Spirit is love, joy, peace, patience, kindness, goodness, faithfulness, gentleness, self-control; against such things there is no law. Now those who belong to Christ Jesus have crucified the flesh with its passions and desires. If we live by the Spirit, let us also walk by the Spirit.

To understand what it means to **"walk in the Spirit,"** it is helpful to examine our physical walk. When we walk physically, we move forward with one foot, start to lose our balance, then catch ourselves with the other foot. We repeat this process over and over again. We could even define a walk as *a successive series of little falls that never happen.* So also, walking in the Spirit is a successive series of falls that don't, or seldom, happen. We say seldom, because even in a physical walk it is possible to occasionally trip and fall. If we do fall in our spiritual walk, we need to "get up off the ground," confess the sin, *know* God has forgiven us, and *knowing* that we are indwelt by the Holy Spirit, *yield* the right of way to Him, and keep walking.

We can learn a lot about walking in the Spirit by examining a physical walk -- a successive series of little falls that never (or seldom) happen.

It is easy to slip into the trap of assuming that our sin is so bad that the Holy Spirit has departed. But God is faithful -- even when we are unfaithful. In Hebrews 13:5, He says, **"I will never desert you, nor will I ever forsake you."** The Holy Spirit did not depart from the men in Corinth who were involved in sin with prostitutes, and He will not leave you. Satan wants you to believe otherwise, but God does not break His promises!

You ask; "How can I learn to walk spiritually?" You can find the answer in how you learned to walk physically -- just like every other little kid. As a toddler, your first few steps were a big event. You probably concentrated very hard to take those first steps. It is a sure thing that you fell on your face a few times. When you did, you bounced right back up and tried again. Quite often, we meet adult believers who have spiritually fallen on their faces, and have been lying there, feeling sorry for themselves, for many years.

Little kids do not learn how to walk by reading a textbook on walking. You could say they learn by "trial and error," or "the school of many falls." They just keep getting back up, trying over and over again, until they develop the skill. That's the same way each of us needs to learn to walk in the Spirit. Do not get discouraged and just lie there if you fall. Get up, off of the ground, confess the sin -- knowing that you are forgiven because of what Jesus did for you on the cross -- and start taking steps -- yielding the right of way in your life to Him and asking the Holy Spirit to take control.

Walk with the Lord, step by step, following the Romans six plan for living: **Know** you are indwelt by the Holy Spirit, because God says you are (not because you feel like you are -- tomorrow you may feel different), then **reckon** it to be true, and **yield** the right of way of your life to Him. Those are three sure steps that will glorify God by producing victory in your life.

Some years ago, I counseled with a young couple at Duke University who were having difficulties in their marriage. When I asked what the problem was, he exclaimed; "Her mother did this." She then responded, "Yes, but his mother did that." The "this" and "that" are not important, except to say that if the mothers really did the "this and that," they were both quite obnoxious! Then the husband and wife continued on with; "My wife did this," and "My husband did that." After listening to the "this's and that's" for about twenty minutes, I turned to the above passage in Galatians, chapter five. We talked about what it was to **"walk in the Spirit"** and the difference between the fruit produced by walking in the Spirit and that produced by walking in the flesh.

We learn to "Walk in the Spirit" in the same way little kids learn how to walk physically -- at "the school of many falls." When they fall, they get up and try again; so also, when we fall we need to confess our sin and keep walking!

I then asked the husband, "Tell me again, what was it your wife's mother did?" The husband instantly, and gleefully, blurted out another example. I then responded by saying; "You know, the really important question is not what your mother-in-law did. Rather, it's how did *you* respond? Was it in the flesh or in the Spirit? If you responded in the flesh, I can imagine your response: **'disputes, dissensions, strife, outbursts of anger.'** But, if you responded by walking in the Spirit, your response was **'love, joy, peace, longsuffering.'"** (That last word, from the King James Version, was not even fair.)

His answer was silence. So I turned to the wife and asked, "What was it your mother-in-law did?" She blurted out an example, and I gave the same response I had given to her husband.

In the remainder of our sessions together, I did little -- other than to remark, "It is not important what the other person did; the important question is 'How did *you* respond? Was it in the flesh or in the Spirit?'"

My purpose was to force them to use the yardstick found in Galatians five to measure whether they were walking in the Spirit or walking in the flesh, and then to suggest that if they were walking in the flesh, they needed to pick themselves up off the floor and yield the right of way to the Holy Spirit. I'm happy to report, they did learn the lesson, and later, went into the ministry.

The important thing is not what the other person did to us. The question we need to ask is: "How did I respond? Was it in the flesh or in the Spirit?

There are times when we need to ask ourselves: "Was my response to what that other person did, in the flesh or in the Spirit?" God gives us a measuring stick to use in making our determination. Just read again Galatians 5:19-23. If you find you are lying on the ground, it's time to get up and start walking, yielded to the Holy Spirit.

There will be times in the life of every believer when the attitudes and behavior expected in our lives will seem impossible. It will be almost as if we are being asked to walk on water. At such times, it is important to remember, that the One who *did* walk on water dwells within you. He gives you His power through the indwelling Holy Spirit to live a life that would otherwise be impossible. He is still in the business of performing what to us seem like miracles. We just need to yield the right of way in our lives to Him and let Him produce the good fruit.

Paul expressed it well, how we should view ourselves, in Galatians, chapter two:

> **"I have been crucified with Christ; and it is no longer I who live, but Christ lives in me; and the life which I now live in the flesh I live by faith in the Son of God, who loved me, and delivered Himself up for me"** (Galatians 2:20).

Many years ago, Bill, a dynamic businessman, was attending a conference at Arrowhead Springs, then the worldwide headquarters for Campus Crusade for Christ. One evening he was standing in the lobby of the hotel, talking to some friends, and the young son of a friend with the last name, Peoples, walked up. Bill patted this young boy on the head and said, "How are you, Peoples?" The boy stopped, faced Bill, pointed his finger right up in Bill's face, and responded, "You're a pimple." Then he repeated it over and over again, "You're a pimple! You're a pimple! You're a pimple."

Bill was embarrassed and felt like he wanted to hide in the carpet. He even thought about how much he would like to take the boy outside for a good spanking. But, instead, Bill managed to muster a smile and said nothing in response.

For the next week, every place Bill would go on the grounds of Arrowhead Springs, he would run into this boy. Young Mr. Peoples would point his finger in Bill's face and say, "You're a pimple!" The boy really had Bill's number. When he would see the boy coming, Bill would try to hide. The worst part of it was that Bill had a room on the fifth floor of the hotel, there was only one elevator, and guess who liked to help the elevator operator? You guessed it. Bill would get on the elevator with other people, and the boy would point his finger up in Bill's face and say, "You're a pimple!" As you might expect, the boy was demolishing Bill's vacation, and Bill developed an intense dislike for him.

The last night of the conference, Dr. Bill Bright, the President of Campus Crusade, spoke on, "How to Love by Faith." The essence of his message was that you are indwelt by the Holy Spirit, and God can love others through you, through the power of the Holy Spirit within you.

The next morning, Bill went to the elevator to go down for breakfast. When he got on the elevator, sure enough there was young Mr. Peoples. Bill started to brace himself, because he knew what was coming. As he did, the message he had heard the night before came to mind. So Bill silently prayed: "God, you love this boy. (He probably added, 'How, I'll never know.') And, Jesus, you live in me. God, I ask you to give me Your love for this boy right now. You love him through me!"

All of a sudden, the boy reached up, grabbed Bill by both hands and asked; "What's your name?" He never again pointed his finger and said, "You're a pimple." It's clear what happened. That young boy instantly felt God's love. In Bill's words, he later said, "God had to use a ten year old boy to teach me how to be a lover!"

For a hard-driving businessman like Bill, God worked a miracle when he changed his attitude toward young Mr. Peoples. Remember, God is in the miracle-working business, and the Holy Spirit can produce within you the fruit of the Spirit, even if someone points their finger in your face and says, "You're a pimple!" So give your faith some legs -- glorify God by living your life walking in the power of the Holy Spirit!

Remember, God is in the miracle-working business, and the Holy Spirit can produce within you the fruit of the Spirit -- even if someone points their finger in your face and says, "You're a pimple!"

Summary of Chapter Twelve:

The New Covenant promised a reconstruction of the heart. God said, "I will put My Spirit within you!" What He has done for believers is greater than a physical heart transplant.

In Peter's sermon on the day of Pentecost, he equated the pouring out of the Spirit with that which had been promised in the Old Testament. In his epistles, Paul explained that the power of the Holy Spirit within us is the *same* power that raised Jesus from the grave.

The secret to having a victorious Christian life is to "walk in the Spirit," knowing we are indwelt by the Spirit, reckoning it is true, and yielding the right of way in our lives to Him. Paul tells us what if we so walk, we will have the fruit of the Spirit.

The important question is not what others have done to us, rather, whether we have responded in the Spirit or in the flesh. If we respond in the Spirit, our response will be **"love, joy, peace, longsuffering, gentleness, goodness, faith, mercy, and temperance,"** in spite of what anyone else does or does not do.

CHAPTER 13
WHERE DO WE GO FROM HERE?

Before moving on to some of the Bible passages that look to the future, we need to say a few things about the interpretation of biblical prophecy. First, I am personally thankful that there is one verse that is <u>NOT</u> in my Bible. It goes, "Believe on the Lord Jesus Christ and have a perfect set of doctrines and thou shall be saved." If that verse were in the Bible, heaven would be a very lonely place, for the interpretation of the Bible's many prophecies for the future is not an exact science. Bible scholars, who agree on other issues, often disagree in their interpretation of biblical prophecy.

INTERPRETATION OF THE Biblical prophecies about end time events is NOT an exact science, and many believers disagree on the particulars. It is imperative that when we disagree we follow Jesus Christ's commandment that we love one another!

Having a correct understanding of Biblical eschatology (the doctrine of last things) is not a prerequisite for getting into heaven, and eschatology should not be an issue that Christians *fight* over. When doctrinal differences arise, we should respect the views of our brothers in Christ, with whom we differ, and remember that God's love for us is not based on *our* having perfect doctrine. We need to always remember Jesus' admonition, **"This is my commandment, that you love one another, just as I have loved you"** (John 15:12).

It is not the purpose of this book to attempt to give a detailed explanation of the events that will surround the second coming of Jesus Christ. (Christian book stores have many other books, written from various perspectives, that do examine the Bible prophecies about the last days.) Rather, our purpose here is to give the readers a general understanding of the entire biblical message so the individual parts, such as end-time prophecies, will be better understood.

It is not by design that the last chapter of this book is numbered *thirteen*. Some people think that thirteen denotes "bad luck," but believers know that such superstitions are not of God. On the other hand, as we examine the Bible's prophecies that look to the future, we find a mixture of *good news* and *bad news*. Good news for those who have trusted in Jesus as their Savior and wait for His glorious return, and bad news for those who have rejected His offer of redemption.

The last book in the Bible, the Revelation of John, is the only book in the Bible that promises blessings for reading it (Revelation 1:3). But, as has often been noted, it does not promise its readers that they will understand it.

The book of the Revelation has 404 verses and at least 280 of them have imagery that can be traced back to the Old Testament, (But no direct quote from the Old Testament.) One could spend a lifetime studying this book and tracing its roots, and still merely scratch the surface in uncovering the truths it conveys. Only a fool would claim infallibility in interpreting its message. But, while there are many passages in the Revelation that are hard to understand, there are some truths that come through loud and clear. For sure, it tells us the future holds different prospects for two groups of people:

And the kings of the earth and the great men and the commanders and the rich and the strong and every slave and free man, hid themselves in the caves and among the rocks of the mountains; and they said to the mountains and the rocks, "Fall on us and hide us from the presence of Him who sits on the throne, and from the wrath of the Lamb; for the great day of wrath has come and who is able to stand?" (Revelation 6:15-17)

After these things I looked, and behold, a great multitude, which no one could count, from every nation and all tribes and peoples and tongues, standing before the throne and before the Lamb, clothed in white robes, and palm branches were in their hands; and they cry out with a loud voice, saying, "Salvation to our God who sits on the throne, and to the Lamb." (Revelation 7:9-10)

Everyone will ultimately identify with one of these passages. Either with those from every nation, who will wave palm branches and rejoice in His presence, or with the many who will try to hide in the rocks to avoid the righteous wrath of His judgment.

The teaching that there will be a future judgment may not be *politically correct* or *culturally popular* among many modern day *"scholars,"* but Paul warns us in I Corinthians to beware of the wisdom of this world: **"Where is the wise man? Where is the scholar? Where is the philosopher of this age? Has not God made foolish the wisdom of this world?"** (I Corinthians 1:20 NIV). Both the Old and New Testaments tell of a coming judgment. The following are but a few of the many passages that refer to the judgment: **"And many of those who sleep in the dust of the ground will awake, some to everlasting life, but others to disgrace and everlasting contempt"** (Daniel 12:2 NASB). **"And it is appointed unto men once to die, but after this the judgment ..."** (Hebrews 9:27 KJV). **"... for we shall all stand before the judgment seat of God. For it is written, 'As I live says the Lord, every knee shall bow to Me, and every tongue shall give praise to God.' So then each one of us shall give account of himself to God."** (Romans 14:10-12).

In light of these passages, we each need to ask ourselves, "Am I ready for the judgment foretold in the Bible?" In light of the Scriptures, there is only one way that we can give an affirmative answer to that question -- by having faith in Jesus Christ as our Savior:

Through the ages, believers have speculated about the nature of their eternal destiny with God. Since our comprehension is limited to things we have perceived in our experience here on earth, Paul tells us our understanding of our eternal state and destiny is also limited: **"Things which eye has not seen, and ear has not heard, and which have not entered into the heart of man, All that God has prepared for those who love Him"** (I Corinthians 2:9). But in I Corinthians fifteen, Paul does tell us some truths about the resurrection that ultimately await those who have placed their faith in Jesus:

But now Christ has been raised from the dead, the first fruits of those who are asleep. For since by man came death, by man also came the resurrection of the dead. For as in Adam all die, so also in Christ shall all be made alive. But each in his own order: Christ, the first fruits; after that those who are Christ's at His coming, then comes the end, when He delivers up the kingdom to the God and Father, when He has abolished all rule and authority and power. For He must reign until He has put all His enemies under His feet. The last enemy that will be abolished is death ...

But someone will say, "How are the dead raised? And with what kind of body do they come?" You fool! That which you sow does not come to life unless it dies, and that which you sow, you do not sow the body which is to be, but just bare grain, perhaps of wheat or of something else. But God gives it a body just as He wished, and to each of the seeds a body of its own. All flesh is not the same flesh: but there is one flesh of men, and another flesh of beasts, and another flesh of birds, and another of fish. There are also heavenly bodies and earthly bodies, but the glory of the heavenly is one, and the glory of the earthly is another. There is one glory of the sun, and another glory of the moon, and another glory of the stars; for star differs from star in glory.

So also is the resurrection of the dead. It is sown a perishable body, it is raised an imperishable body; it is sown in dishonor, it is raised in glory; it is sown in weakness, it is raised in power; it is sown a natural body, it is raised a spiritual body. If there is a natural body, there is also a spiritual body. So also it is written: "The first Adam became a living soul." The last Adam became a life giving

spirit. However, the spiritual is not first, but the natural; then the spiritual. The first man is from the earth, earthy, the second man is from heaven. As is the earthly, so also are those who are earthy; and as is the heavenly, so also are those who are heavenly. And just as we have borne the image of the earthly, so shall we bear the image of the heavenly.

Now I say this brethren, that flesh and blood cannot inherit the kingdom of God, nor does the perishable inherit the imperishable. Behold, I tell you a mystery; we shall not all sleep, but we shall all be changed, in a moment, in the twinkling of an eye, at the last trumpet; for the trumpet will sound, the dead will be raised imperishable, and we shall be changed. For this perishable must put on imperishable, and this mortal must put on immortality. But when this perishable will have put on the imperishable, and this mortal will have put on immortality, then will come about the saying that is written, "Death is swallowed up in victory. O death, where is your victory? O death, where is your sting?" The sting of death is sin, and the power of sin is the law; but thanks be to God, who gives us the victory through our Lord Jesus Christ. (I Corinthians 15:20-57)

One of the inevitable experiences of this life is seeing our physical bodies deteriorate as we age. When one is young and energetic, it is hard to comprehend the physical changes that will come through the years. But, they do overtake all of us. What a wonderful promise we have that this is but a temporary experience. For the wise, the experience of growing old serves as a warning of our physical mortality, and a reminder that we need to be prepared for the time when we will stand before the Lord.

The Scriptures give us explicit warnings. In many passages the judgment is associated with the regathering of Israel back to the Promised Land. Joel 1:15 (NASB) speaks of this, "Alas for the day! For the day of the Lord is near, and it will come as destruction from the Almighty." Joel chapter two described it as, "There has never been anything like it, nor will there be again after it.... The day of the Lord is

indeed great and very awesome ..." (Joel 223 and 2:11 NASB). Joel also warns **"For behold, in those days and at that time; when I restore the fortunes of Judah and Jerusalem, I will gather all nations, and I will bring them down to the valley of Jehoshaphat, and I will enter into judgment with them there, on behalf of My people and My inheritance Israel, whom they have scattered among the nations"** (Joel 3:1-2 NASB).

Earlier in chapter seven, this book looked at prophecies that pointed to Jesus as the Messiah, and noticed that many of the Messianic prophecies <u>seem</u> to be contradictory -- that there are contrasting prophecies, often mixed together. One passage pictures the Messiah as a suffering servant who will be **"despised and rejected of men,"** while another pictures Him as a glorious King to whom **"every knee will bend."** Another passage describes Him as being the Savior who will **"pour out His soul as an offering for sin,"** but this contrasts with a prophecy that describes Him as a mighty King who will conquer. Another describes Him as being **"cut off"** from His people Israel, but there is another that proclaims **"He will not fail."** One prophecy foretells the Messiah will present Himself on the back of a donkey, while another pictures Him as a majestic king when He comes to judge the world.

If one were to read the biblical prophets without the benefit of hindsight, it would be easy to conclude that God promised *two* Messiahs. Today we see the prophecies do not picture two Messiahs. Rather, they pictured *one* Messiah who will come *two* different times. First, He came as the suffering servant, **"He was despised and we esteemed Him not,"** and **"thou shalt make His soul an offering for sin."** (Isaiah 53:3 & 10 KJV)

In the New Testament we learn that after Jesus died on the cross, He rose from the grave, but before he ascended into heaven, He promised that He would later return to the earth. When He does return, He will reign as the majestic, righteous King, and *every* knee will bow before Him. But, many Christians believe the Bible teaches that He will not merely return as the Christ for Christians, but, at that time, the Israelites will also recognize that He is their Messiah.

We need to return to two powerful passages that we looked at in Chapter seven, as we consider this important truth:

"And I will pour out on the house of David and on the inhabitants of Jerusalem, the spirit of Grace and supplication, so that they will look on Me whom they have pierced, and they will mourn for Him as one mourns for an only child ..." (Zechariah 12:10 NASB). **"Afterward the sons of Israel will return and seek the Lord their God and David their king; and they will come trembling to the Lord and to His goodness in the last days"** (Hosea 3:5 NASB).

There are many Christians who are in agreement with most of the interpretive issues in this book, but will differ with me on the question of Israel's place in God's plan for the future. While I appreciate the sincere commitment to Christ of many who differ with me on this issue, I do believe an understanding of Israel's place in the prophetic picture is critical as we consider the coming judgment, so I will explain my viewpoint.

AN UNDERSTANDING of ISRAEL's PLACE IN THE PROPHETIC PICTURE is CRITICAL WHEN diGGING INTO THE BiblE's VIEW of THE FUTURE.

Some believers assume that since the Jews rejected Jesus as their Messiah, that they are no longer part of God's program for the future. But, the prophet Jeremiah foretold that in the **"*latter days*"** there will be a time of judgment from God on the evil of this world, followed by God fulfilling the **"intent of His heart"** toward Israel:

Behold the tempest of the Lord! Wrath has gone forth, a sweeping tempest; it will burst on the head of the wicked. The fierce anger of the Lord will not turn back, until He has performed, and until He has accomplished the intent of His heart; in the *latter days* you will understand this. "*At that time*," declares the Lord, "I will be the God of all the families of Israel, and they shall be my people." (Jeremiah 30:23 - 31:1 NASB, italics supplied)

The prophet Jeremiah further stated that God will never forsake the nation of Israel. Read what the Lord says through

Jeremiah in chapter thirty-three:

"Behold days are coming," declares the Lord, "when I will fulfill the good word I have spoken to the house of Israel and the house of Judah. In those days and at that time I will cause a righteous Branch of David to spring forth; and He will execute justice and righteousness on the earth. In those days Judah will be saved and Jerusalem shall dwell in safety; and this is the name by which she shall be called; the Lord is our righteousness." For thus says the Lord, "David shall never lack a man to sit on the throne of the house of Israel ..."

And the word of the Lord came to Jeremiah saying: "Thus says the Lord: 'If you can break My covenant for the day, and My covenant for the night, so that day and night will not be at their appointed time, then My covenant may also be broken with David My servant that he shall not have a son to reign on his throne, and with the Levitical priests, My ministers. As the host of heaven cannot be counted, and the sand of the sea cannot be measured, so I will multiply the descendants of David My servant and the Levites who minister to Me.

And the word of the Lord came to Jeremiah saying, "Have you not observed what this people have spoken, saying 'The two families which the Lord chose, He has rejected them?' *Thus they despise My people, no longer are they a nation in their sight.* Thus says the Lord, 'If My covenant for day and night stand not, and the fixed patterns of heaven and earth I have not established, then I would reject the descendants of Jacob and David My servant, not taking from his descendants ruler over *the descendants of Abraham, Isaac and Jacob. But I will restore their fortunes and have mercy on them.'"* (Jeremiah 33:11-26 NASB, italics supplied)

Jeremiah wrote during a time of apostasy, just before the children of Israel were taken captive to Babylon because of their disobedience. Jeremiah described their rebellious behavior at that time as "indeed the sons of Israel and the sons of Judah have been doing only evil in My sight ... have been only provoking Me to anger by the works of their hands" (Jeremiah 32:30 NASB). Yet, even at a time when their works were evil, God proclaimed that the future existence of the

nation (*descendants of Isaac and Jacob, not merely Abraham --
implying the nation of Israel*) is as sure as the fixed order of the
universe.

The author of this book believes that the Old Testament
teaches there are conditions as to *which* generation of the
descendants of Jacob will inherit the land promised in the
Abrahamic Covenant, but there are no conditions given as to
whether God's complete promise to Israel will ultimately be fulfilled. It therefore follows that there will someday be a group of
Israelites who will accept Jesus as their Messiah who will inherit the Promised Land.

ThERE will ulTimATEly bE A GROUP of IsRAELiTES
who will inHERiT THE PROMisEd LANd.

The New Testament also teaches this truth. After giving
his great doctrinal dissertation in Romans, chapters one
through eight, the Apostle Paul turns to the issue of Israel in
chapters nine through eleven. It is important to remember,
Paul was writing after Jesus was rejected by Israel and they had
Him crucified. In this section of Romans, Paul first asserts that
the promises of the Abrahamic covenant are not to *all* who are
natural descendants of Abraham:

**But it is not as though God's word has failed. For they
are not all Israel who are descended from Israel; neither are
they all children because they are Abraham's descendants,
but: "Through Isaac that your descendants will be named."
That is, it is not the children of the flesh who are children of
God, but the children of the promise are regarded as descendants** (Romans 9:6-9). In the following chapters, Paul wrote,
**"But as for Israel He says, 'All the day long I have stretched
out My hands to a disobedient and obstinate people'"**
(Romans 10:21 - obviously talking about the nation of Israel and
not the church) and then continues, **"I say then, 'God has not
rejected His people, has He?' May it never be!"** (Romans 11:1).
Continuing on, figuratively describing Israel as a branch that is
broken off of an olive tree, Paul asserts that the broken branch

will, in the future, be grafted back into the *tree:*

> **But if some of the branches were broken off, and you** (writing to Gentiles) **being a wild olive, were grafted in among them and became partakers with them of the rich root of the olive tree, do not be arrogant toward the branches ... it is not you who supports the root, but the root supports you. You will say then, "Branches were broken off so that I might be grafted in." Quite right, they were broken off for their unbelief, and you stand only by faith.... And they also, if they do not continue in their unbelief, will be grafted in; for God is able to graft them in again.... how much more shall those who are the natural branches** (Israelites) **be grafted into their own olive tree.** (Romans 11:17-24)

Paul then closes out this section of Romans exhorting his readers: **For I do not want you, brethren, to be uninformed of this mystery, lest you be wise in your own estimation, that a partial hardening has happened to Israel until the fullness of the Gentiles has come in. And thus all Israel will be saved, just as it is written: "The deliverer will come from Zion; He will remove godlessness from Jacob. And this is My covenant with them when I take away their sins." From the standpoint of the gospel they are enemies for your sake, but from the standpoint of God's choice they are beloved for the sake of the fathers** (Abraham, Isaac, and Jacob), **for the gifts and calling of God are irrevocable.** (Romans 11:25-29)

While the above passage does not specifically refer to the land, the Old Testament Prophets repeatedly promised to re-gather Israel in the last days, and Jesus, looking to the future, said, **"Jerusalem will be trampled under foot by the Gentiles, until the times of the Gentiles be fulfilled"** (Luke 21:24).

A literal interpretation of the Bible ultimately leads to the view that God will fulfill His promise to Abraham, Isaac, and Jacob about the land. For many centuries, this was hard for Christians to believe, because it looked like it was a political and military impossibility. But, in recent years this view has gained followers because the Jews have regained control of the Holy Land *and Jerusalem* -- in spite of what appeared to be insurmountable obstacles preventing the fulfillment of this prophecy. (Though they do not yet have ALL of the land promised them in the Abrahamic Covenant.)

If God has revoked the promise of the land, it must be assumed it is because of the children of Israel's disobedience to the Mosaic Covenant, or because of their rejection of Jesus as Messiah. If it was revoked because of disobedience to the Mosaic Covenant, that would violate the principle in Galatians 3:17: **"The law which came 430 years later, does not invalidate a covenant previously ratified by God, so as to nullify the promise."** If it was revoked because of Israel's rejection of Jesus as Messiah, why did Paul *later* assert, **"God has not rejected His people whom He foreknew"** (Romans 11:2).

There is no statement in the Scriptures that God's promise of the land has been revoked because of Israel's rejection of Messiah. Luke tells us in the last chapter of his gospel, **"Then He opened their** (the disciples') **minds to understand the scriptures"** (Luke 24:45). Acts 1:3 records that after the resurrection, Jesus appeared to the disciples for forty days **"and speaking the things concerning the kingdom of God."** After having their minds opened, and being personally taught by Jesus, the disciples then asked Him, **"Lord, is it at this time You are restoring the kingdom to Israel?"** (Acts 1:6).

If one assumes that the promise of the land has been repealed because of the rejection and crucifixion of Jesus by Israel, one must assume that the disciples did not learn from Jesus during those forty days of personal instruction when **"He opened their minds."** Their question assumed that there will be a time when the Old Testament promises, which included the land, will be fulfilled for the nation of Israel. This indicates that the disciples believed the promises in the Abrahamic Covenant were still future for Israel. It is significant that Jesus did not correct them when they asked that question.

The question of Israel's place in God's plan for the future of the world ultimately goes back to whether the covenant God made with Abraham was conditional or unconditional. Since we have seen that it became unconditional when Abraham believed God, we can assume the Abrahamic Covenant will be completely fulfilled irrespective of what any individual does.

But, for the natural descendants of Abraham (the Israelites), the promise of the land is conditional as to which generation will respond in faith and be part of the fulfillment.

Earlier this book looked at the amazing prophecy in Daniel nine that foretold when the Messiah would come the first time -- at the end of sixty-nine weeks of years. The prophecy in Daniel said a total of seventy weeks of years are decreed for the Israelites, **"to put an end to sin, to atone for wickedness, to bring in everlasting righteousness, to seal up vision and prophecy, and to anoint the most holy"** (Daniel 9:24).

In Matthew twenty-four, when the disciples asked Jesus about the end-times, He described an event He referred to as **"the abomination of desolation which was spoken of through Daniel the prophet"** (Matthew 24:15). In Daniel's prophecy, the abomination of desolation is part of the seventieth week. Jesus warned that there will be a time of "great distress" on the earth, and that He will return to earth, with power and great glory, immediately after the events surrounding the abomination of desolation. (Matthew 24:15-31)

The pieces fit together perfectly if we understand the seventieth week of Daniel as a future event. It is hard to place it in the past, because Jesus said, in Matthew 24:29-31, that He would return (immediately) at the end of it. As Daniel's seventieth week, this time of great distress and desolation is a period of seven years of 360 days each, divided into two equal parts of 1260 days, by an event described as, **"And one who causes desolation will place abominations on a wing of the temple"** (Daniel 9:27). Since the same lengths of time are repeated in the book of Revelation, chapters eleven through thirteen, it is only natural to assume that the books of Daniel and the Revelation are describing events that will take place during the same time period. At the end of the seventieth week, the message from Gabriel in Daniel foretold that sin will end, and everlasting righteousness will be brought in. The Revelation gives us the same promise.

Ezekiel thirty-seven uses a vision to proclaim that, in *the last days*, God will restore his chosen people, Israel, in spite of their being spiritually dead -- as dead as a valley of dead, dry bones.

Read how Ezekiel reported the vision the Lord gave him:

The hand of the Lord was upon me, and He brought me out by the Spirit of the Lord and set me in the middle of a valley; it was full of bones. He led me back and forth among them, and I saw a great many bones on the floor of the valley, bones that were very dry. He asked me, "Son of man, can these bones live?" I said, "O Sovereign Lord, you alone know." Then He said to me, "Prophesy to these bones and say to them, 'Dry bones, hear the word of the Lord! This is what the Sovereign Lord says to these bones: I will make breath enter you, and you will come to life. I will attach tendons to you and make flesh come upon you and cover you with skin; I will put breath in you, and you will come to life. Then you will know that I am the Lord.'"

So I prophesied as I was commanded. And as I was prophesying, there was a noise, a rattling sound, and the bones came together, bone to bone. I looked, and tendons and flesh appeared on them and skin covered them, but there was no breath in them. Then He said to me, "Prophesy to the breath; prophesy, son of man, and say to it, 'This is what the Sovereign Lord says: Come from the four winds, O breath, and breathe into these slain, that they may live.'" So I prophesied as He commanded me, and breath entered them; they came to life and stood up on their feet -- a vast army. Then He said to me: "Son of man, *these bones are the whole house of Israel.* They say, 'Our bones are dried up and our hope is gone; we are cut off.'

Therefore prophesy and say to them: 'This is what the Sovereign Lord says: O my people, I am going to open your graves and bring you up from them; I will bring you back to the land of Israel. Then you, My people, will know that I am the Lord, when I open your graves and bring you up from them. I will put my Spirit in you and you will live, and I will settle you in your own land. Then you will know that I the Lord have spoken, and I have done it, declares the Lord.'"

The word of the Lord came to me: "Son of man, take a stick of wood and write on it, 'Belonging to Judah and the

Israelites associated with him.' Then take another stick of wood, and write on it, 'Ephraim's stick, belonging to Joseph and all the house of Israel associated with him.' Join them together into one stick so that they will become one in your hand. When your countrymen ask you, 'Won't you tell us what you mean by this?' Say to them, 'This is what the Sovereign Lord says: I am going to take the stick of Joseph -- which is in Ephraim's hand -- and of the Israelite tribes associated with him, and join it to Judah's stick, making them a single stick of wood, and they will become one in my hand.'

Hold before their eyes the sticks you have written on and say to them, 'This is what the Sovereign Lord says: *"I will take the Israelites out of the nations where they have gone. I will gather them from all around and bring them back into their own land. I will make them one nation in the land, on the mountains of Israel.* There will be one king over all of them and they will never again be two nations or be divided into two kingdoms. They will no longer defile themselves with their idols and vile images or with any of their offenses, for I will save them from all their sinful backsliding, and I will cleanse them. They will be My people, and I will be their God.

My servant David will be king over them, and they will all have one shepherd. They will follow My laws and be careful to keep My decrees. *They will live in the land I gave to my servant Jacob, the land where your fathers lived.* They and their children and their children's children will live there forever, and David My servant will be their prince forever.

I will make a covenant of peace with them; it will be an everlasting covenant. I will establish them and increase their numbers, and I will put my sanctuary among them forever. My dwelling place will be with them; I will be their God, and they will be My people. Then the nations will know that I the Lord make Israel holy, when My sanctuary is among them forever.'" (Ezekiel 37:1-28 italics supplied)

It is clear from this passage in Ezekiel, and in others, that immediately before God restores Israel to the Promised

Land, the Israelites will still be scattered among the nations of the world and will be spiritually destitute. But, the Old Testament Prophets repeatedly foretold there will be a time when Israel will be gathered back to the land. Ezekiel's vision tells us that at that time the Israelites will experience new life.

We have previously looked at Hosea's prophecy that there will be a period of time when Israel **"will live many days without a King"** ... but that **"afterward the sons of Israel will return and seek the Lord God and David their king ... in the last days"** (Hosea 3:4-5 NASB). After being rejected, Jesus expressed the same idea when He proclaimed, **"Did you never read in the Scriptures: 'The stone which the builders rejected, this has become the chief cornerstone; This came about from the Lord, and it is marvelous in our eyes'? Therefore, I say to you, the kingdom of God will be taken away from you and be given to a nation producing the fruit of it. And he who falls on this stone will be broken to pieces, but on whomever it falls, it will scatter him like dust."** (Matthew 21:42-44)

Jesus also lamented, **"O Jerusalem, Jerusalem, who kills the prophets and stones those who are sent her! How often I wanted to gather your children together, the way a hen gathers her chicks under her wings, and you were not willing. Behold, your house is being left to you desolate! For I say to you, from now on you shall not see Me until you say, 'Blessed is He who comes in the name of the Lord'"** (Matthew 23:38-39). The clear inference of this statement is that there WILL be a time in the future when the Jews will say, **"Blessed is He who comes in the name of the Lord."**

We also saw in Zechariah chapter twelve that, in the last days, Israel will be back in the land with all the surrounding nations making war against them, and they (the children of Israel) will **"look upon Me whom they have pierced."** The context of this prophecy about Israel is a time when **"And I shall bring them back, because I have had compassion on them; ... I will whistle for them to gather them together, for I have redeemed them; and they will be as numerous as they were before."** (Zechariah 10:6-8)

For centuries, skeptics scoffed at the Bible's prophecies that the Holy Land would again be occupied by a regathered nation of Israel. They asserted that it was not only improbable, it was also politically and militarily impossible. From a human perspective, they were right.

In 1948, the day after David Ben Gurion declared Israel an independent state, on a tiny piece of land, the Arab nations attacked and gleefully announced that they were going to annihilate all of the Jews in Palestine. The Arabs had 650,000 men -- equipped with the best weapons and air power that oil money could buy. The Israelites had a 45,000 man defense force, weapons for only 2 out of 3 members, a three days supply of ammunition, and 20 unarmed Piper Cubs (during the war, some Jews from Europe flew in some obsolete German Messerschmit fighter planes).

When the war ended, the Jews were not merely survivors, they had expanded their territory, and they had captured half of Jerusalem. Later, in the Six Day war of 1967, the Jews gained control of the rest of the Holy City.

Many Bible scholars believe that the return of the control of Jerusalem to Israel is preparatory for the second coming of Jesus. In Matthew 24:36, Jesus told us no one knows the day or hour when He will return, so it is impossible to know *for sure*. But, while we can't know the day or hour, we are told to watch for the season (Matthew 24:32-33).

During the end-time events, Israel will be attacked by the surrounding nations (Zechariah 12), but apparently, just before those days, there will be concerted peace efforts. Paul wrote to the believers in Thessalonica: **"Now as to the times and epochs, brethren, you have no need of anything to be written to you. For you yourselves know full well that the day of the Lord will come like a thief in the night** (unexpectedly). **While they are saying, 'Peace and safety!' then destruction will come on them suddenly, like birth pains upon a woman with child, and they shall not escape."** (I Thessalonians 5:1-3)

Describing events during the end-times, Jesus said, **"But when you see Jerusalem surrounded by armies, then rec-**

ognize that her desolation is at hand ... these are days of vengeance in order that all things which are written may be fulfilled ... and Jerusalem will be trampled under foot by the Gentiles until the times of the Gentiles be fulfilled ... And there will be signs in sun and moon and stars, and upon earth dismay among nations ... men fainting from fear and expectation of the things which are coming upon the world, for the powers of the heaven will be shaken. And then they will see the Son of Man coming in a cloud with power and great glory. (Luke 21:20-27)

ISRAEL'S PARTIAL RETURN TO THE LAND, ITS REGAINING CONTROL OF JERUSALEM, THE EXTREME HATRED OF THE JEWS BY THE SURROUNDING NATIONS, AND FALSE HOPES OF PEACE IN THE HOLY LAND, ARE ALL FACTORS THAT WILL BE PRESENT WHEN THE TIME OF TESTING AND JUDGMENT COMES FOR THOSE WHO DWELL UPON THE EARTH.

In Ezekiel's vision of the dry bones, we read that when the "bones" initially come together there will be **"no breath in them."** If we are living in the period of time that immediately precedes "the end-times," then this description of Israel from Ezekiel 37:8 is where we are right now.

We have seen a partial regathering of Israel. Thus far, this return has taken place without the Israelite's realization that Jesus is the Messiah -- they are still rejecting Him. Before Jesus establishes His Kingdom on the earth, God will breathe spiritual life into those "dry bones." As Romans 11:26 tells us, there will be a time when **"... And thus all Israel will be saved ... The Deliverer will come from Zion."**

When Jesus, the Deliverer, comes, the Jews will **"... look on Me, the one they have pierced; and mourn for Him"** (Zechariah 12:10). **"And one will say to Him, 'What are these wounds between your arms?' Then He will say, 'Those with which I was wounded in the house of my friends'"** (Zechariah 13:6). **"They will call on My name, and I will answer them; I will say, 'They are my people,' and they will say, 'The Lord is our God'"** (Zechariah 13:9).

As one reads the many Scriptures that reiterate that God's promises to Israel will be fulfilled in spite of Israel's long history of rebellion and disobedience, it is easy to respond that Israel is not entitled to such gracious treatment. But, we need to remember that God's offer of salvation to all of us was **"while we were yet sinners"** (Romans 5:8). *All believers* should be thankful that God's grace is truly amazing.

When Israel recognizes her Messiah, people from all the nations of the world will also see God's glory:

"I will display my glory among the nations, and all the nations will see the punishment I inflict and the hand I lay upon them. From that day forward the house of Israel will know that I am the Lord their God. And the nations will know that the people of Israel went into exile for their sin, because they were unfaithful to Me.

So I hid My face from them and handed them over to their enemies, and they all fell by the sword. I dealt with them according to their uncleanness and their offenses, and I hid My face from them.

Therefore, this is what the Sovereign Lord says: ' I will now bring Jacob back from captivity and will have compassion on all the people of Israel, and I will be zealous for My holy name. They will forget their shame and all the unfaithfulness they showed toward Me when they lived in safety in their land with no one to make them afraid.

When I have brought them back from the nations and have gathered them from the countries of their enemies, I will show Myself holy through them in the sight of many nations. Then they will know that I am the Lord their God, for though I sent them into exile among the nations, I will gather them to their own land, not leaving any behind. I will no longer hide My face from them, for I will pour out My Spirit on the house of Israel,' declares the Sovereign Lord." (Ezekiel 39:21-29)

The prophets Isaiah and Habakkuk both foretell that there will be a time when the whole world will see **"the glory of the Lord"**:

For the earth will be filled with the knowledge of the glory of the Lord, as the waters cover the sea.
Isaiah 11:14 & Habakkuk 2:14

Both the Old Testament and the New Testament tell us there will be a time when every knee will bow to the Lord:

"Turn to Me and be saved, all you ends of the earth; for I am God, and there is no other. By Myself I have sworn, My mouth has uttered in all integrity a word that will not be revoked: before Me every knee will bow; by Me every tongue will swear. They will say of Me, 'In the Lord alone are righteousness and strength.' All who have raged against Him will come to Him and be put to shame" (Isaiah 45:22-24).

For we shall all stand before God's judgment seat. For it is written, "As as I live," says the Lord, "every knee shall bow to Me; And every tongue shall give praise to God." So then, each one of us shall give an account of himself to God. (Romans 14:10-11)

Therefore also God highly exalted Him, and bestowed on Him the name which is above every name, that at the name of Jesus every knee should bow, of those who are in heaven and on earth and under the earth, and that every tongue should confess that Jesus Christ is Lord, to the glory of God the Father. (Philippians 2:9-11)

If you have not yet bowed the knee to Jesus, do not delay. Now is the time for salvation. God promises that when you come to Him you will be satisfied. Jesus said, **"I am the bread of life, he who comes shall not hunger, and he who believes in me shall never thirst"** (John 6:35).

We are living in a time when many believers are watching and waiting for the return of the Lord. With the partial return of the Jews to the land, their political control of Jerusalem, and the great animosity of the neighboring people toward Israel, the prophetic stage is set like never before in the history of the world.

As we watch and wait for His return, we have a job to do! We need to proclaim the Good News -- that through Jesus people can find eternal life; have their names written in the Book of Life; and escape the judgment the Bible tells us will come upon this world. As we wait for His return, each of us needs to remember John's exhortation:

And now little children, abide in Him, so that when He appears we may have confidence and not shrink away from Him in shame at His coming.

(I John 2:28)

The Bible begins with the fall of man. The rest of the Bible unfolds God's progressive revelation of the redemption He offers to us through Jesus, His promised Messiah. It is only fitting that we should end this book with some awesome passages from the last three chapters of the final book of the Bible, the Book of the Revelation. No book has ever closed with more powerful words than these. Any comments I might make about these passages would be, at best, superfluous. So, I let them speak for themselves:

Then I saw a great white throne and Him who was seated on it. Earth and sky fled from His presence, and there was no place for them. And I saw the dead, great and small, standing before the throne, and books were opened. Another book was opened, which is the book of life. The dead were judged according to what they had done as recorded in the books. The sea gave up the dead that were in it, and death and Hades gave up the dead that were in them, and each person was judged according to what he had done. Then death and Hades were thrown into the lake of fire. The lake of fire is the second death. If anyone's name was not found written in the book of life, he was thrown into the lake of fire. (Revelation 20:11-15 NIV)

Then I saw a new heaven and a new earth, for the first heaven and the first earth had passed away, and there was

no longer any sea. I saw the Holy City, the new Jerusalem, coming down out of heaven from God, prepared as a bride beautifully dressed for her husband. And I heard a loud voice from the throne saying, "Now the dwelling of God is with men, and He will live with them. They will be His people, and God himself will be with them and be their God. He will wipe every tear from their eyes. There will be no more death or mourning or crying or pain, for the old order of things has passed away."

He who was seated on the throne said, "I am making everything new!" Then He said, "Write this down, for these words are trustworthy and true."

He said to me: "It is done. I am the Alpha and the Omega, the Beginning and the End. To him who is thirsty I will give to drink without cost from the spring of the water of life. He who overcomes will inherit all this, and I will be his God and he will be my son. But the cowardly, the unbelieving, the vile, the murderers, the sexually immoral, those who practice magic arts, the idolaters and all liars - - their place will be in the fiery lake of burning sulfur. This is the second death." (Revelation 21:1-8)

Then He told me, "Do not seal up the words of the prophecy of this book, because the time is near. Let him who does wrong continue to do wrong; let him who is vile continue to be vile; let him who does right continue to do right; and let him who is holy continue to be holy."

"Behold, I am coming soon! My reward is with Me, and I will give to everyone according to what he has done. I am the Alpha and the Omega, the First and the Last, the Beginning and the End."

"Blessed are those who wash their robes, that they may have the right to the tree of life and may go through the gates into the city. Outside are the dogs, those who practice magic arts, the sexually immoral, the murderers, the idolaters and everyone who loves and practices falsehood."

"I, Jesus, have sent my angel to give you this testimony

for the churches. I am the Root and the Offspring of David, and the bright Morning Star."

The Spirit and the bride say, "Come!" And let him who hears say, "Come!" Whoever is thirsty, let him come; and whoever wishes, let him take the free gift of the water of life.

I warn everyone who hears the words of the prophecy of this book: If anyone adds anything to them, God will add to him the plagues described in this book. And if anyone takes words away from this book of prophecy, God will take away from him his share in the tree of life and in the holy city, which are described in this book.

He who testifies to these things says, "Yes, I am coming soon." Amen. Come, Lord Jesus. The grace of the Lord Jesus be with God's people. Amen.

(Revelation 22:10-21 NIV)

INDEX OF SCRIPTURES

(Chapters in bold print, pages where verses are located in parentheses)

OLD TESTAMENT PASSAGES:

(New Testament references on the following page)

NEW TESTAMENT PASSAGES:

Matthew 4 (83, 84), **6** (119, 121), **7** (85), **10** (85-86),
    11 (87, 93), **13** (88-89), **16** (83, 89- 91, 107, 110), **18** (120),
    21 (91, 145), **22** (91-94, 107), **23** (75, 146), **24** (143, 146)

Mark 10 (56)

Luke 3 (73), **12** (88), **19** (74, 80), **21** (141, 146), **22** (101-102)
    24 (1, 142)

John 1 (56, 65, 83, 90, 125), **3** (58, 103, 135), **6** (85, 149),
    8 (85), **11** (85), **14** (1), **15** (133)

Acts 1 (21, 142), **2** 104, 124), **3** (81, 104-105), **4** (76), **7** (78-77),
    13 (105)

Romans 3 (51), **4** (33), **5** (25, 106, 148), **6** (54, 113-114), **7** (52)
    8 (135) **9** (140), **10** (140), **11** (140-142, 147), **14** (135, 149)

I Corinthians 1 (134-135), **2** (135-136), **6** (125-126),
    15 (136-137)

II Corinthians 3 (76)

Galatians 1 (12) **2** (129, 131), **3** (49-52, 142), **5** (126, 128), **6** (120)

Ephesians 1 (125), **2** (58), **4** (119)

Philippians 2 (65-66, 69, 149), **3** (13-14)

Colossians 1(58)

I Thessalonians 5 (147)

II Timothy 2 (151), **3** (13)

Hebrews 6 (31), **8** (57, 100), **9** (54, 100-101, 103, 135),
    10 (102, 111), **11** (34), **12** (134), **13** (33, 127)

James 2 (35)

II Peter 1 (11, 13, 115-116)

I John 1 (116-117), **2** (117-119, 149), **5** (58, 109)

The Revelation 1 (134), **6** (134), **7** (134), **20** (150),
    21 (150 - 151), **22** (151)

Epilogue

In Matthew 28:18-20 Jesus gave His followers the Great Commission, when He said:

All power is given unto Me in heaven and in earth. Go ye therefore, and teach all nations, baptizing them in the name of the Father, and of the Son, and of the Holy Spirit: Teaching them to observe all things whatsoever I commanded you: and lo, I am with you always, even unto the end of the world.

It is often assumed that the command in the Great Commission is to *go*. Actually, a conjugation of the word translated *go* indicates that it could be translated "as you are going." The imperative in this command is to teach, or as some translations render it, to "make disciples." Jesus knew that every day each believer would be going someplace and that His followers would be spread to the ends of the world. The imperative command is that whenever and wherever each of us ventures, we have an assignment to share the Good News about Jesus, and to thus make disciples who will follow Him. My prayer is that readers of this book will use the knowledge they have gained in reading it to communicate the Gospel to others.

I have also written a book titled, *As You are Going... Make Disciples*. It is a collection of short stories, each one selected to communicate a truth that will help the readers be more effective as they fulfill their responsibility "as they are going." It's ISBN number is 0-9657835-4-5 and it is available through the internet at www.hisbride.org/books.htm or through any Christian Bookstore. I trust that you will find it an entertaining read, and that reading it will help you be more effective as you share your faith in Jesus with others.

Bob Prall, Author